LOVE AND ANGER

GEORGE F. WALKER

Coach House Press Toronto

Great North Artists Management, Inc.
350 Dupont Street
Toronto, Ontario, Canada M5R 1V9

Cover photo: Peter Blais as Petie Maxwell and Nancy Beatty as Sarah Downey in the Factory Theatre production of *Love And Anger* at the Factory Theatre in Toronto, October 1989.

The punctuation of this play carefully adheres to the author's instructions.

Published with the assistance of the Canada Council and the Ontario Arts Council.

Canadian Cataloguing in Publication Data

Walker, George F., 1947–
    Love and anger

A play
ISBN 88910-369-0

I. Title.

PS8595.A44L68 1990   C812'.54   C90-093891-9
PR9199.3.W34L68 1990

Introduction

For many who attended the premiere of *Love And Anger* at Toronto's Factory Theatre on October 11, 1989, George F. Walker's newest play hit a sensitive nerve. The standing ovation at the end of the show brought to a climax an emotional response that galvanized the audience like an electrical charge throughout the two-hour production. Despite its frequent laughter, the audience reacted with something akin to a collective knee-jerk – a response more appropriate to a smart slap than a comic *coup*. Spilling downstairs into the Factory's cabaret after the performance, people argued heatedly about the changes reshaping Toronto and its theatre. Like a conduit, *Love And Anger* generated animated discussion about the ways that art and politics work in Canada's largest city – a subject that the audience seemed eager to address.

At the time, I was too busy enjoying myself to reflect on why. Only later did I consider that many in the audience might have shared the sense of release and renewal that I experienced that evening. Watching Walker's characters vent their anger at a system of power that left them feeling impotent and isolated, I faced my own frustrations with the city that I now call home. *Love And Anger* helped me focus my feelings about Toronto at a time when the city and my responses to it had grown maddeningly complex. Judging from the enthusiastic reactions that the production continued to elicit, *Love And Anger* provided a similar service for a lot of other people.

Six months after it opened, *Love And Anger* was still filling the factory's 300-seat theatre most nights of the week – an unprecedented success for this not-for-profit theatre that has fought an uphill battle against the pressures of Toronto's escalating economy. In a feature article in *The Globe and Mail* on February 3, 1990, theatre critic Ray Conlogue tried to explain why *Love And Anger* was so successful. After interviewing a variety of audience members, he concluded that "a lot of

Introduction

Torontonians have lately become angry and upset about
the direction their city is going in...." Conlogue
suggested that in Petie Maxwell, the play's central
character, they had finally found their voice.

It requires less investigation to confirm a more
practical point: with *Love And Anger* the Factory Theatre
generated a welcome infusion of cash. That this theatre
should use Walker's newest play to successfully
introduce its 20th season and continue its battle with
the bank was very appropriate. Not only had it
produced Walker's first play, *The Prince of Naples*, in
1971; since its opening in May 1970, the Factory has
produced more of Walker's plays than any other theatre,
providing him with the loyal support and reliable
resources that have helped him develop into a major
talent.

The success of *Love And Anger* validated the Factory's
commitment to George F. Walker in the best way
possible, and at just the right time. Besides helping the
company balance its budget, the play reaped artistic
dividends for Toronto theatre at a point when many of
its practitioners were experiencing creative as well as
fiscal enervation – a bonus that boosted the Factory's
cachet along with its capital both inside and outside of
the theatre community. Although Toronto's profile as a
theatre centre had increased significantly during the
1980s, this was primarily due to the promotion of non-
indigenous work – shows such as *Cats*, *Les Misérables*
and *The Phantom of the Opera* that had commercial
producers proclaiming the birth of a world-class theatre
market in the city's downtown core. For many in
Toronto's theatre community, the success of *Love And
Anger* proved that alternatives to the mega-hits still
were viable. Even more important, it confirmed what
they had long felt possible: a Canadian play could do
just as well as an import, providing it was allowed time
to run – the time necessary to establish financial
credibility as well as critical clout.

Although few people, least of all Walker himself,
anticipated the positive impact of *Love And Anger* on

Toronto's changing theatre scene, anyone monitoring the evolution of Canadian theatre over the last 20 years might have predicted it. By the time *Love And Anger* opened, Walker had firmly established himself as one of Canada's most important creative assets. The previous year, his seventeenth play had been his biggest hit: *Nothing Sacred,* an irreverent reworking of Turgenev's *Fathers and Sons,* won a Governor General's Literary Award in Canada, where it received numerous productions across the country; in the United States its production at the Mark Taper Forum in Los Angeles turned up on *Time* magazine's list of the year's 10-best shows. Indeed, *Nothing Sacred* had been so successful that many people wondered what Walker would do to follow it. Would he write another adaptation? Would he remount one of his earlier plays? Would he try something altogether new?

Walker responded with a resounding affirmation of his personal roots by returning to the territory of *The East End Plays* – a series of interconnected comedies set in Toronto's East End that he wrote just prior to *Nothing Sacred.* In writing *Love And Anger,* the playwright revisited the neighbourhood of his youth and reclaimed the emotional landscape of his most socially committed work. In the preface to *Nothing Sacred,* Walker acknowledged that *The East End Plays* represent a reconciliation between the nihilism of his earlier work and his mounting commitment to social change. He explained: "If you forget that your work, and all your indignation and your anger, comes from the way people are being treated – the so-called victims – then you can't talk to the victims, and your feeling for them is useless."

In his most recent plays, Walker seems increasingly concerned to "talk to" the people whom Petie, in *Love And Anger,* characterizes as "the troubled and the marginal." What is so reassuring about the response to *Love And Anger* is that it indicates that a lot of other people want to listen. While *The East End Plays* were successful, the interest they generated was significantly less than that elicited by *Love And Anger.* Perhaps

the audience for these plays had been like Eleanor
Downey, Petie's middle-class secretary in *Love And
Anger* who is reluctant to join his cause; it needed to be
pulled into Petie's fight for a fairer world despite its
"better" judgement. Or, perhaps like Gail Jones, the black
woman who comes to Petie for help when her husband
is put in jail, the audience needed to be convinced that
it has the power to win its pursuit: "Just trust me," Petie
admonishes Gail early in the play; "Trust yourself for
wanting to trust me. Trust the picture in my mind. But
most of all, trust the anger we both feel about the
injustice you're suffering. Because the anger is the only
thing we really need."

Petie's speeches in *Love And Anger* echo many of the
comments that Walker has made in interviews during
the last few years. In the preface quoted above, for
example, he states: "You begin with anger and energy;
but then you face things – the details of life – and you
meet the emptiness that you're afraid of. I think that's
true in my work, and it's probably true in my life." As a
result, it's tempting to read the character of Petie
Maxwell in *Love And Anger* as a persona for Walker
himself – a development of Paul Gallagher, the character
in *Beautiful City* (the last of *The East End Plays*) who
Walker has acknowledged expresses many of his own
ideas about life and work.

Like Paul, who has come to hate his work as an
architect, Petie undergoes an identity crisis directly
related to his profession; unlike Paul, he emerges from
the crisis spiritually reborn. In Scene One, Petie explains
his perception of his past life to Eleanor as they sit
alone in his basement office in a rundown area of the
city: "I was a lawyer. I defended the obviously guilty.
And the obviously not guilty. ... It was death." A
debilitating stroke has caused Petie to re-evaluate his
relationship with the social institutions he has taken for
granted, and to recuperate the values he lost during law
school. Like Paul who, in *Beautiful City*, is led to
consider that his work is used by others to devalue both
art and life, Petie has been led to question the purpose

of his work as a lawyer. He asks Eleanor: "Where did it get us. Where did it get the world. What did we accomplish."

In both *Beautiful City* and *Love And Anger* the male protagonists turn to women in an attempt to find the answers they seek – women who offer them a way through the morass of anger, guilt and moral confusion they have created in their lives. In *Beautiful City*, Paul connects with Gina Mae Sabatini, a prescient check-out clerk in a discount store who wants "a throbbing, connecting, living, creative neighbourhood" in which to raise her daughter – and is prepared to use violence to get what she wants. In *Love And Anger*, Petie joins forces with Eleanor's schizophrenic sister, Sarah Downey, as well as Gail Jones; together, he believes they can "change the world."

Not coincidentally, Gail, like Gina Mae, brandishes a gun before *Love And Anger* concludes, reminding the men responsible for her husband's incarceration that "I'll use it. If you make me mad again I'll find you and put it against your head and pull the trigger." Such violence, however, and the anger with which it is fueled, are overtaken by love in the play – and by the strength that love brings to the characters who trust in its healing power. While this assertion of love as an antidote to social injustice may seem ineffectual to some, for others it is as necessary an ingredient for change as anger. Petie recognizes that his "new era" of "getting even" must include compassion as well as vengeance if it is to effect lasting reconcilation. In the last scene of the play, his adversary, John "Babe" Conner, is tried for more than the positions he promotes in his newspaper. Petie explains that Conner also is tried "for his endless manipulative use of the lowest common denominator and his lack of respect for the essential mysteries of life."

For the characters in this play, these mysteries include the ability of love to overcome isolation and fear – love which combines with anger to become a viable force for good. For me, such mysteries are more than romantic delusions when they can be seen to have practical effects. In the case of the production of *Love And Anger,* these are tantamount to a small miracle. Walker's love and anger with the city of his birth have provided regenerative inspiration for its theatre community. The success of his exuberant production of the play offers a new model for the structuring of indigenous production in Canada. It now is possible to envision a future in which Canadian plays no longer are restricted to subscription series in not-for-profit theatres where they must close after a four- or five-week run. It even is possible to consider that a subsidized theatre might be able to produce one Canadian play as a way of financing others.

Robert Wallace
Toronto, April 1990

Love And Anger

Love And Anger premiered in a production by Toronto's
Factory Theatre on its mainstage on October 11, 1989
with the following cast:

PETER 'PETIE' MAXWELL, *Peter Blais*
GAIL JONES, *Dawn Roach*
ELEANOR DOWNEY, *Clare Coulter*
JOHN 'BABE' CONNER, *Benedict Campbell*
SEAN HARRIS, *Hardee T. Lineham*
SARAH DOWNEY, *Nancy Beatty*

Directed by George F. Walker
Production designed by Peter Blais
Lighting designed by Peter Freund
Music composed by Lesley Barber

Persons

PETER 'PETIE' MAXWELL, *50*
GAIL JONES, *early 20s*
ELEANOR DOWNEY, *mid-40s*
JOHN 'BABE' CONNER, *late 40s*
SEAN HARRIS, *early 50s*
SARAH DOWNEY, *late 30s*

Place

A damp grimy office in the basement of an old building on the fringe of the downtown area. Contains a desk, several chairs, a small couch, a few filing cabinets. There are a few small windows looking onto the street above. There are several metal bookcases half-filled with books. There are more books in several cartons on the floor. There is a tiny outer office stage left. The door to this office usually remains open, but we should see only a small portion of it. And there is a conveyor belt which runs up the wall, under the windows, to a trap door leading to the street.

Note: An intermission could be placed between Scenes Four and Five.

Scene One

PETER 'PETIE' MAXWELL, *a fifty-year-old in an often worn,
slightly rumpled, quality suit. Loose tie. Glasses. Sitting
behind his desk. Fiddling with a cigarette.* GAIL JONES,
*twenty-two, in jeans and a baseball jacket, sits in a chair
in front of the desk*

MAXWELL The law is vulgar. Just like religion. Vulgar things both of
them. Institutions corrupted by their own self-
importance. I'm immune to their seductive power. I've
been around too long. Seen a lot of so-called illegal
activity. Seen too much of it to believe it's just deviant
behaviour. Anyway, more times than not, these days I
come down in favour of the deviants. I'm not talking
about the violent now. Especially not about the sexually
violent. Violent sexual deviants I've got no time for. I
don't want them executed or anything, but I think we
have to construct a system of mutual protection. Us
from them. And them from themselves. I'm in favour of
increased government spending in the area of prison
reform, medical facilities for the criminally
dysfunctional. That sort of thing. You follow me so far?

GAIL No.

MAXWELL I'm talking about your situation vis-à-vis my situation.

GAIL Nothing you've said in the last half hour has anything to
do with my situation. I just want my husband out of
prison.

[MAXWELL *stands. Leans against the desk*]

MAXWELL I was talking about the law. Trying to let you know that
even though I'm constrained by it, I'm not impressed by
it. The law is vulgar in its rigidity. Insensitive to the
nuance of human existence. Derived and constructed
from knowledge within a narrow historical corridor. In
short, it's in love with itself. You'll get no true
satisfaction from the law. You're marginal. Your cause is
marginal. Outside the corridor, so to speak.

GAIL He's innocent.

[MAXWELL *picks up a cane which is lying on his desk. And
starts to move around. He has a slight limp. During the*

13

course of the play he sometimes uses his cane,
sometimes he doesn't]

MAXWELL More and more I hear that word less and less. I spend a
lot of time in courtrooms and I can tell you that that
word has definitely fallen out of fashion. It even makes
some judges cringe. I advise you not to use the word
'innocent' in front of anyone with real power.

GAIL He didn't break into those places the way they say he
did.... I mean he did. But he didn't want to. He was
forced.

MAXWELL I know. I've read the transcript. I was impressed by your
testimony. I believe you when obviously no one else
does. That's why I called you back. I just want to make
the situation clear.

GAIL You're not. It's not clear. You're failing at making it clear.

MAXWELL It's complex. I'm expressing the complexity before I
attempt the clarification. Any fool could rob the
situation of complexity and then clarify an essentially
fraudulent simplicity.

GAIL Okay. Do that. I don't mind. I won't hold it against you.

MAXWELL Well there's our problem. We have two situations here.
Yours of course is the one most urgent. But mine is the
more persistent. You want your husband out of prison. I
want to undermine the entire institutional bias of our
culture. Now I believe it's possible we have a
serendipitous union of intention here but you'll have to
allow me to proceed in my own way.

GAIL And what will that be. Your way?

MAXWELL Trickery. I'm going to deke the legal establishment right
out of its pants. For example. You say he was forced to
make those break-ins by a couple of seedy hoods. Now
normally I'd have to prove that. But quite simply that's
impossible. We'd have to get the hoods to testify against
themselves. No doubt they're stupid men but even that
kind of hopeless maudlin stupidity has limits. No, I
favour a solution that would involve blackmailing a
judge with some invented indiscretion. Getting him to
grant an appeal to save his own reputation. Perhaps
even getting him to recommend a financial
compensation for wrongful imprisonment. More and

14

more I've come to believe you have to take money away from these people and their system in order to be truly satisfied. I mean it's the thing they and their system value most.

GAIL I've got to ask you a question now. Don't take it the wrong way. Are you a ... crooked lawyer.

MAXWELL In the strictest meaning of that term, yes. But remember the strictest meaning is the meaning of the strict – i.e. the law. The better truth is that I'm one of the few revolutionaries in Western civilization. A hidden force. You have, in a sense, hitched your wagon to a political imperative. We are about to become history in the making. How do you feel about that.

GAIL Not too good, really.... Sounds like trouble. I don't want trouble. I just want my husband out of jail.

MAXWELL Don't you want a shiny new future ... for you and your husband.

GAIL Yes. I do.

MAXWELL And what about the rest of the marginals. The millions of others in your situation. Or in situations even worse.

GAIL What about them.

MAXWELL If you could, would you help them.

GAIL I guess.

MAXWELL You're a good soul. I could tell from the heartbeat of your testimony. The love you have for your husband is just one arm of a many-armed beast. Full of compassion for everything in the world that needs love. Am I right.

GAIL *Are* you right.

MAXWELL I hope I'm right. Trust me. Do you trust me.

GAIL No.

MAXWELL Do you *want* to trust me.

GAIL Yes.

MAXWELL That's a start.
[*A light is turned on in the outer office*]
Eleanor. Could you come in here for a moment, please.
[MAXWELL *returns to the desk. Sits on the edge. Near* GAIL]
Can you write.

GAIL What do you mean.

MAXWELL Can you read. Can you write.

GAIL Sure. What kind of a question is that.

15

MAXWELL Please don't be offended. I see lots of people who can't you know. Illiteracy is a problem.

GAIL Yeah, well it's not my problem.

[ELEANOR DOWNEY *comes in. She is middle-aged. A bit younger than* MAXWELL. *Conservatively dressed. Carrying a bag of cleaning supplies*]

ELEANOR Can I help you with something, Mr. Maxwell.

MAXWELL Eleanor. This is Gail Jones. Gail. This is Eleanor. Eleanor works with me. She's part of my team, my movement.

ELEANOR I'm his secretary.

MAXWELL That's her cover. She's actually the heart and soul of my operation.

ELEANOR I'm just his secretary. [*to* MAXWELL] Please. I've asked you before. Don't involve me in whatever it is you're up to these days. I have problems of my own.

MAXWELL [*to* GAIL] She doesn't trust you. When she trusts you she'll tell you the truth about herself.

ELEANOR Please.

MAXWELL Gail. I want you to go with Eleanor. She'll make a little space for you at her desk. She'll give you a pen and paper. She'll give you a coffee, although strictly speaking that's not part of her job, and she'll help you if you're having any difficulty completing your task.

GAIL I have a task? Listen I don't –

MAXWELL I want you to write about yourself. And your husband.

GAIL About the break-ins?

[MAXWELL *reaches into his desk drawer. Takes out a chain of coloured paper clips. Begins to finger them*]

MAXWELL Yes. Eventually. But don't start there. Start earlier. Write about your lives. Your needs. Your fears. Your beliefs.... Tell your story. Don't worry about style, structure, resolution. I can work on that later. Just think of it as a first draft. Something from deep inside the heart. Let it resonate. You know what I mean by resonate?

GAIL I know what resonate means!

MAXWELL So let it resonate.

[MAXWELL *is adding paper clips to the chain*]

GAIL [*to* ELEANOR] Is he really a lawyer.

ELEANOR Well he was once one of the most brilliant in the country. But he's had a.... Yes. He's a lawyer.

[ELEANOR *goes to* MAXWELL. *Grabs the paper clips from him*]

GAIL [*to* MAXWELL] If I do this. This writing. Will it help you get Dave out of prison.

MAXWELL I'd rather not answer that question right now.

[GAIL *looks at* ELEANOR]

ELEANOR Don't worry, Gail. I'm sure Mr. Maxwell knows what he is doing. Go into my office, dear. I'll be with you in a minute.

[GAIL *leaves.* ELEANOR *turns. Sits opposite* MAXWELL]

Did you take your medication.

MAXWELL Yes. Yes I did. Don't worry. I actually do know what I'm doing. We are now officially embarked upon phase two. Do you want me to explain phase two for you.

ELEANOR What was phase one.

MAXWELL The obvious. I was a lawyer. I defended the obviously guilty. And the obviously not guilty. You typed. You answered the phone. You prepared affidavits. Where did it get us. Where did it get the world. What did we accomplish.

ELEANOR It was a job. We did our jobs.

MAXWELL It was death. Death was surrounding us like a demon inevitability. I suffered a stroke. It was something I could have done without, but I decided to turn it to my advantage. My brain is new. The stroke ... and ... [*he takes another chain of paper clips from his pocket*] ... a little therapy, gave me a new brain.

ELEANOR The stroke actually destroyed part of your brain.

MAXWELL Well it was a part I didn't need anyway. My ability to communicate wasn't affected. My ability to communicate was somehow enhanced.

ELEANOR That could be a matter of opinion. In any event, medically speaking, you're an invalid.

MAXWELL Medicine is number four on my hit list. Right after law, religion, government.

ELEANOR How did religion get on that list. Religion is a comfort to many people, myself included.

MAXWELL I'm not talking about all religions. Just the religions of fear.

ELEANOR Are we discussing phase two now.

Peter Blais (Maxwell) and Clare Coulter (Eleanor)

MAXWELL We're in the preamble.... And what about you. Your life is in pieces. Tiny pieces. Shattered glass. Here and there. Random. Nothing but a –

ELEANOR Please.

MAXWELL Your sister. I was speaking about your sister. We have to help Sarah. She's part of it. She'll be included. She's your problem. She's my problem. She's society's responsibility.

ELEANOR She's schizophrenic. She can't be helped. She can only be monitored. They've convinced me.

MAXWELL They?

ELEANOR The doctors.

MAXWELL Never let them convince you. Their confidence is spellbinding. But it's just there to hide their disappointment. Trust me. [*he hugs her*] Please don't give up on her.

ELEANOR I'd better go check on Gail.

MAXWELL Gail.... She's a good soul. Her husband was framed, shafted, railroaded. She's an issue. She's a cause.

ELEANOR She's a human being. And she's scared about what's happened to someone she loves. You scare her too. I don't think you should talk like that to her anymore. Talk like you used to talk to your clients.

MAXWELL I patronized them. I pissed on their ingrained intelligence.

ELEANOR Sometimes that's better.

[*She leaves.* MAXWELL *hears something up in the street. Gets a chair. Takes it over under the window. Stands on it. Taps on window*]

MAXWELL Hey. You. Get out of that garbage. There's nothing in that garbage you want. Have a little self-respect. Come on! Self-respect! Try it out!

[*A commotion in the outer office.* JOHN 'BABE' CONNER *comes in. In his late forties. Well dressed*]

CONNER Are you Peter Maxwell.

MAXWELL They used to call me Peter. They call me Petie now.

[ELEANOR *comes in. Visibly upset*]

ELEANOR I want to call the police about this man. He laid hands on me.

MAXWELL [*advancing on* CONNER] You should be shot! In primitive

19

societies they had exquisite rituals of pain designed for people like you. [*to* ELEANOR] Didn't they.

ELEANOR I don't know.

MAXWELL [*to* CONNER] What's wrong. Some trouble with mummy!? A little kindergarten Freudian encounter with a distant but alluring teacher? We don't care!

CONNER She was in my way. She wouldn't move. I just helped her back into her chair. Control yourself, man.

MAXWELL You're a bully. I hate you! She hates you too! Call the police, Eleanor.

ELEANOR Good idea.

[*She leaves*]

CONNER You people are pretty sensitive. I don't want the police involved. Don't you know who I am. Don't you recognize me.

MAXWELL Sure. You're John Conner. I read your newspaper every day. It's painful. But I figure someone has to monitor the crap you publish.

CONNER Yeah I know how you feel about my paper. The whole city knows how you feel about my paper. That's why I'm here.

MAXWELL Not so fast. You owe my associate an apology. On second thought we'll take money. One hundred dollars.

CONNER I'm not giving you any money. You're a clown. People told me you were probably just some kind of deranged clown. And they were right.

MAXWELL Two hundred dollars. And fast. Eleanor's on the phone.

CONNER No way.

MAXWELL You physically assaulted my associate. A respectable woman with an unblemished record of public and private service.... It will make the front page. Not in your paper of course. The front page of your paper is reserved for inflammatory headlines and pictures of people tormented by agonizing personal grief. Three hundred dollars!

CONNER What makes you think I can be.... [*he looks toward the outer office*] Two hundred.

MAXWELL Put it on the desk.

[CONNER *pulls a roll of bills from his pocket. Peels a couple of bills off the pile. Tosses them on Maxwell's*

desk. Sits in Maxwell's chair. MAXWELL *puts the money in his jacket pocket. Picks up his phone. Pushes a button*]
Eleanor. You call the police yet?... Well call them back. Tell them it *might* have been a mistake. I'll keep you posted.... You're in my chair by the way. How's Gail doing.... Well she's probably all tied up by syntax. The hell with syntax. Tell her that for me. [*hangs up*]
[MAXWELL *looks at* CONNER. CONNER *stands*]
So what can I do for you, Babe. That's what your friends call you, isn't it. Babe? Because you love baseball. Right?

CONNER We have a problem. You and I have a problem. It's getting out of hand.

MAXWELL How's that, Babe.

CONNER Well in the first place –

MAXWELL Want to sit down, Babe?

CONNER In the first place, we know you're responsible for defacing our street boxes.

MAXWELL That's a serious charge. [*he takes a can of spray paint from a desk drawer. Slams it down on the desk*] You have proof?

CONNER Of course I've got proof. What do you think I'm doing here!

MAXWELL I don't know. Maybe you came here to beat up my secretary. Maybe your secretary's on vacation. Maybe she's in the hospital –

CONNER God, man. What's wrong with you. You talk like a ... you talk like a dope addict.

MAXWELL How the hell would you know how a dope addict talks. You want to find out. Hang around. Twenty percent of the people who come through that door are dope addicts. Look I haven't got time for small talk. What's your problem.

CONNER You. Your personal little war against my newspaper. I want it to stop.

MAXWELL Close the paper down. It'll stop then.

CONNER Who do you think you are. I'm a businessman. I'm a legitimate publisher. I have rights. My company has rights.

MAXWELL Your paper is a fascist rag. It panders to everything weak and uncertain and uninformed in the human race. It has the rights given to it by a society which is essentially indifferent to the weak, uncertain and uninformed. I no longer recognize this society or its governing body. I am a citizen of the new era. I call this the age of getting even. Your newspaper is history. I'm just getting started.... You want to take action against me, go ahead. A public battle in court is just what I want. You get me charged with vandalism, or whatever. I turn the trial into a holy war.

CONNER   I have options.

MAXWELL   Could you be more specific.

CONNER   I have options. I didn't get where I am by letting people push me around. I have ... options. I'm talking about things you might find personally hazardous.

MAXWELL   Of course you are. You're a Nazi.

CONNER   Hey watch your mouth. Where do you get off, using a word like that to describe me. You know what that word means to people?

MAXWELL   Deep in my heart. At the root of my tenuous connection to the essence of life, I believe you are a Nazi. Your particular place in the historical corridor allows you to modify your behaviour for appearances, but you are still a Nazi. If you were put in a position of power in any society desperate for a violent purging you'd buy yourself a uniform – and you'd be a Nazi!

CONNER   I told you to watch your mouth! I hate that word, I just hate it.

MAXWELL   You see a few months ago I had occasion to stare into the benign eye of God. And as God shrugged and gestured sadly for me to come rest in purgatory for eternity unless I got my priorities straight, I made myself some promises. And this is one of them. If it looks like a Nazi, call it a Nazi!!

CONNER   You're in big trouble. You may be insane. But that won't save you. Get ready for the battle of your life.

[CONNER *grabs the can of spray paint. Leaves*]

MAXWELL   Good advice.

[GAIL *comes in*]

GAIL   Are you too busy to talk.

MAXWELL   Never. How are you doing.

MAXWELL Yeah. Well, I couldn't think of any other designation. I'm working on it.

HARRIS Are you all right. Are you fully recovered. Should you be drinking so much.

MAXWELL Yes to all those questions.

HARRIS Where's Eleanor.

MAXWELL I don't know. Out buying cleaning supplies probably. She's desperate to find something to remove the grime in this place.

HARRIS Who's that girl out there at her desk. A client?

MAXWELL A friend.

HARRIS I miss you, Peter. The other partners miss you.

MAXWELL I'm touched. Tell them I'm touched for me.

HARRIS Of course they're perplexed. They don't understand why you left.

MAXWELL They don't understand why people don't all wear suits the same colour. They don't understand why some young people still fall in love without asking each other what their job prospects are. They don't 'understand' anything except their work. And they don't see that their work is part of a systematic oppressive machine which conspires to deprive people of the options and the knowledge which are their fundamental rights.

HARRIS Have you become a communist or something. [*laughs*]

MAXWELL Yes.

HARRIS A communist?

MAXWELL Or something.

HARRIS You're talking about your former partners like they're soulless monsters. Most of those men have been your friends for twenty years.

MAXWELL That wasn't me. My body was invaded by some external force. It happened in my second year at law school. Late at night in the library. I removed pages from a reference book with my Exacto knife. And do you know why.

HARRIS Sure. So no one else could get access to them. So you'd do better. Place higher. We all did it, Peter.

MAXWELL Up to that point in my life I had never done anything remotely like that. My parents brought me up to prize honour. Honour was a big thing to them. The force made me do it. The force was everything in our world. Ambition, competition, self-promotion. Powerful,

25

seductive things made by their power and seductiveness into a living external entity. *It* entered me. *It* removed the pages from that book. *It* helped me graduate head of my class. Start that damn firm. Hire all those damn clones. Pretend to be their friend. It's dead now. I'm back! I'm reborn. I'm like a little kid – still half-formed. But I'm growing. Fast. Do you understand what I'm talking about.

HARRIS   Yes.

MAXWELL   You do? Really? Don't humour me now, Sean. Do you really get what I'm saying here.

HARRIS   Well ... I think so. Yes. You're looking for some kind of renewal. Some kind of – what's that word ... spiritual ... spiritual renewal.

MAXWELL   Good for you. So will you come work with me here? Get reborn? Start all over again.

HARRIS   No. Of course not. I'm going to enter politics. Run federally. I'm announcing my candidacy tomorrow evening at the office. I'd appreciate it if you didn't come. There's a party afterward at the club. You're welcome to attend *that* if you're ... in the mood.

MAXWELL   That's what you came here to tell me.

HARRIS   I came here because you asked for a meeting.

MAXWELL   But you're a conniving bastard. You never go anywhere without your own agenda.

HARRIS   I was about to remind you how long we've been friends. But of course that wasn't really you was it.

MAXWELL   The small part of me that wasn't the external force. The small part that was still human always had a soft spot for you.

HARRIS   Really.

MAXWELL   Yeah. I think it's because basically you were unmotivated. Your privileged background, your inherited wealth somehow shielded you from the vile needs of others.

HARRIS   You mean I had charm.

MAXWELL   Yes. You were charming, in a very basic way. Charm isn't necessarily a bad thing.... Have another drink.

HARRIS   No. I'm fine.

MAXWELL   So.... Politics.... Interesting. Why.... Boredom?

HARRIS Probably. Yes.

MAXWELL I suppose you think that's reason enough.

HARRIS Basically, yes ... I mean once you've attained a certain amount, climbed to the top of the mountain so to speak, even if you've had assistance, you take the opportunity to look around. Find new challenges ... new mountains so to speak. I'm still young. Still have something to – what's the word ... contribute. But of course you don't agree.

MAXWELL Hmmm. Let's just say that there are certain areas of life where charm ceases to be ... charming ... and becomes ... well, disgusting. One might even say immoral. There are problems in this country, Sean. In the world. We expect our politicians to solve them. Perhaps you think that's naive.

HARRIS Yes I do. Not without some genuine albeit sentimental romantic justification. But naive nevertheless.

MAXWELL You'll probably get elected.

HARRIS The climate seems right. I'm told my timing is good.

MAXWELL You have a platform?

HARRIS I have an issue.

MAXWELL What is it.

HARRIS The deficit, of course.

MAXWELL Of course.... Anything else?

HARRIS If we bankrupt the country all the rest is more or less meaningless. Even with your new philosophy, whatever it is, surely you must still understand that the economy is everything.

MAXWELL The economy as it stands. As you and your kind define it.

HARRIS Is there some other way of defining it. Are you talking about redistribution or something.

MAXWELL Or something.... So you don't want me at your side when you announce. People will be puzzled. We've been a team a long time.

HARRIS The word's out about you, Peter. Nothing tangible. Just rumour. Most of it tied to your stroke.

MAXWELL They think I'm demented.

HARRIS Your behaviour in the last couple of months has been more than a bit eccentric. People haven't been blessed

27

Peter Blais (Maxwell) and Hardee T. Lineham (Harris)

with a personal audience like I have. They don't know
that you are 'reborn.' They think that maybe you're still
very ill. This conflict with Babe Conner –

MAXWELL Nazi!

HARRIS Excuse me?

MAXWELL He's a Nazi. He must die…. In a manner of speaking I
mean. He must be laid to rest. And his influence with
him.

HARRIS That might be difficult.

MAXWELL His newspaper is a cancer on the body politic.

HARRIS It's tacky yes. Badly written. Sensationalist. Even
regressive. But well … who do you think reads that
paper. Our people don't even give it a glance…. Your
people read it.

MAXWELL My people? Your people? Let's keep the distinctions a
bit more abstract for now Sean. We don't want a class
war here, do we. I mean all I'm looking for is a little
damage control. An easing up on the exploitation.
Getting him to stop taking dead aim at the lowest
common denominator.

HARRIS He's a client.

MAXWELL Conner? Since when.

HARRIS He engaged us this morning.

MAXWELL Tricky bastard…. So he's suing me.

HARRIS That's an option. There are several ways that option
could be handled. You've left yourself wide open here
Peter.

MAXWELL Libel?

HARRIS That's an option. I'm considering the possibilities.

MAXWELL You personally? You haven't litigated in years. Look, why
don't you let someone else in the firm handle it,
especially if you're going to run for public office. The
heat I'm planning to generate from this thing could
seriously damage you. This thing is bigger than that
little rag of Conner's. This is the first step in the
reorganization of an entire culture! This is the beginning
of the end of the secret societies!

HARRIS Knock it off. It's a civil suit. And you're dead meat.
You've been harassing the guy. You've put it in writing in
his competitors' papers. You've talked about it on

cheesy talk-shows. You've scrawled it across his billboards and his street boxes. You've written outrageous, bullheaded, unsupportable, inflaming crap about this guy, and you've signed your name. You're defenceless.

MAXWELL I have no assets.

HARRIS Bull.

MAXWELL I gave everything away. The house, car, stocks, everything.

HARRIS Come on. You don't seriously expect me to believe that.

MAXWELL On an impulse. Pure. And childlike.... It's all gone. I'm immune. I have nothing. Except my name. And I'm changing my name.

HARRIS Why. Are you going into hiding.

MAXWELL Just the opposite. Anyway I'm not changing my last name. I'm changing my first name. I want people to call me Petie. Not Peter. Petie!

HARRIS Why.

MAXWELL Petie Maxwell. It sounds better. Younger. More unfinished. Like me.... The way I am now. Call me Petie! Try it!

HARRIS Are you drunk. Have you just slipped over the edge here, or what. We were talking about a possible law suit.

MAXWELL You were threatening me. I know the routine. I just wanted to let you know it wouldn't work. Go tell Conner it didn't work. If you're lucky he'll fire you. Trust me. You don't want to be associated with him. He's going down. The name calling, that's just the beginning. This man has done many nasty, illegal things. And I've got the stuff that's eventually going to prove it.

HARRIS What do you mean by 'stuff.' You mean hard evidence?

MAXWELL I'm talking about a certain kind of ... information.

HARRIS What.

MAXWELL Can't tell. Privileged. For now.

HARRIS How'd you get it.

MAXWELL Just sat here. People came through that door and gave it to me. I moved my operation down to this sad and nearly forgotten part of the city, opened for business, and all sorts of quasi-exotic creatures came through my door. Most of them pathetic. Many of them helpless.

Some of them purely evil. But they all had stories. We're
talking about the dregs here, Sean. And some of them
are privy to a lot of very damaging information. And they
came in here and talked. About themselves mostly.
About things that pertained to their own severe
dilemmas. Arrested for drugs, arrested for petty theft,
armed robbery, soliciting – the whole miserable gamut.
But some of the names, the places, in their histories
were from another world. I just wrote them down. Had
them write them down. Conner's name came up quite a
bit. Some of it rumour. A story overheard. That kind of
thing. But that kind of thing can be followed up.
Checked out. No one ever did before, that's all. No one
ever burned inside enough, needed to grow enough. But
then there was me. Trust me. Get him to fire you. He's
going down. And so are some others. It's all part of
phase two. The amazing rebirth of Petie Maxwell and
the new era to which he is dedicated....
[*Pause*]
[HARRIS *stands. Calmly puts his drink down on the table*]

HARRIS   So I have your word that you won't be there for my
announcement tomorrow.

MAXWELL   Yes.

HARRIS   Good. Well it's been great seeing you again.
[*He puts out a hand.* MAXWELL *looks at it oddly. Then
takes it. They shake. Continue to hold hands.* HARRIS *looks
at his watch*]
Well I better run. I'm taking Sandra and the kids out to a
movie.

MAXWELL   Very generous of you.

HARRIS   Is that a joke. I didn't get it.

MAXWELL   You don't 'take' your wife out to a movie anymore. You
go together. I read that in a magazine a while ago. The
magazine said married people became happier that
way.

HARRIS   Too bad you're not still married to her yourself. You
could check that theory out personally.

MAXWELL   The man I used to be didn't deserve a good marriage.
Even to a jerk like Sandra. How are my kids by the way.

HARRIS   They're not your kids. They're mine. Remember?

MAXWELL See what I mean. You'd been screwing my wife since law school and it took me twenty years to find out. I must have been a very distracted man. Did I ever tell you how much it hurt me when I found out about you and Sandra.

HARRIS No.... You're not going to tell me now are you.

MAXWELL It killed me a bit. It darkened my life. Made me feel like one of God's lowest creatures. A maggot under a rock. Made me throw up a lot. I threw up for six months.

HARRIS I'm ... you know ... sorry.

MAXWELL Can I kiss you.

HARRIS What ... I don't understand.

MAXWELL I just want to kiss you.

HARRIS On the mouth?

MAXWELL No actually. I'd like you to drop your pants. I want to kiss your ass. No really, it's important to me. I feel it's a way of finally completing my humiliation. Can I do that.

HARRIS No you can't.

MAXWELL Will you kiss mine then. In some ways that would be better. If I drop my pants would you give me a long wet kiss on my ass.

HARRIS You're in deep trouble Peter. You should seek professional help.

MAXWELL Relax. It was just a passing thought.

HARRIS Right. Well. I really do have to be leaving.

MAXWELL Go ahead.

HARRIS You'll have to let go of my hand first. You're squeezing it.
[*Pause*]
[MAXWELL, *still holding* HARRIS' *hand, gets very close to his face*]

MAXWELL Don't even think about it! Don't consider it for even one minute. If you are stupid enough to take what I've told you to Conner so you can make some Brownie points, I want you to put this into the gains and losses equation. I know stuff about you too. All those years of doing business together, Sean. The little shortcuts you sometimes took.

HARRIS And you too.

MAXWELL Yes. But I'm repenting. And what's more important ... I'm immune. Remember?

HARRIS No one's immune. That's self-delusion. There are still things in this world you care about. People you care about. There's no way you got rid of everything. Now let go of my hand.
[MAXWELL *obeys. Steps back*]
Thank you.

MAXWELL Goodbye, Sean.

HARRIS Goodbye ... Petie.
[HARRIS *leaves.* MAXWELL *grabs a book. Throws it at the door*]
[*Pause*]

MAXWELL He's dangerous. I can't believe how dangerous he's become. He'll go to Conner. They'll form a pact. An ungodly alliance.... Is this the focal point.... Is this going to be a holy war. Is it?
[MAXWELL *walks over to the window. Looks out*]
[*Blackout*]

Scene Three

ELEANOR, GAIL, *and* SARAH DOWNEY.

SARAH *is Eleanor's sister. A woman in a loose housecoat. Gym shoes. A knapsack on her back. Sitting cross-legged on the desk. Talking while the other two listen.* GAIL *is enthralled.* ELEANOR *is nervous, impatient*

SARAH Big tractor trailers. Hundreds of them. All painted white. Everything white. White tires. Hundreds of big white tractor trailers thundering down the highways. Looking for adventure. Looking for a place to take over. Surround. A small town, surrounded by tractor trailers is every small town's worst nightmare. And these guys know it. The guys who drive these things. Big beefy white guys who bought these tractor trailers and painted them white. Sold their houses to buy them, sold their Harley-Davidsons and their kids' roller skates, made their wives become prostitutes and cashed their baby bonus cheques, so they could buy their tractor

33

trailers and form a club. A club that was big and fast and
white and thunders down any highway to any
destination and takes over. [*jumps off desk*] Big beefy
mean white guys who hate little people. And little cars.
But mostly they hate black people, and brown people
and yellow people. So they surround a town and they
take it over and they become the power. They're
indestructible. They're armour-plated. They're full of
hate. And now they've got a headquarters. A centre of
operations. First thing they do is kill everyone who isn't
beefy or white. Kill all the skinny people. And the two
black people in town. And the old guy who owns the
Chinese restaurant. Kill them openly. Kill them without
fear. Because they're in control. They're free to be
themselves. Free to be the one thing that's been hidden
all these years. The big beefy mean white guys full of
hate. Because some of them, most of them, aren't really
big, don't look big, only have the big guy *inside* them.
The big beefy guy inside them has been talking to them
for years. Telling them to let him out. To do his thing.
His necessary thing. First get me a machine he says. A
big thundering machine, an operations base, a mobile
base, a tractor trailer. Get it rollin'. Get some respect.
Join up with others. Declare ourselves. Then get a
permanent home.... So they did. They got a town. They
got it surrounded. And word gets out. Soon it starts to
spread. Thousands of white tractor trailers banding
together. Taking over towns. Killing little people, brown
people, everyone who isn't beefy and white. It's a
movement. It's happening everywhere. It's out in the
open. It's an accepted thing. It's the way it is. We're
surrounded. It's our turn to die....
[*Pause*]

GAIL Because we're not big and beefy? [*she laughs*]

SARAH Because we're not white. Because we're black.
[GAIL *looks at* ELEANOR]

ELEANOR Gail *is* black, Sarah.

SARAH Yeah. That's right. I know she's black. That's why I'm
sharing this secret information. This information is for
the ears of our people only.

Love And Anger

GAIL [*to* ELEANOR] I don't get it.

ELEANOR Sarah and I are black too, Gail. Perhaps you haven't noticed. I mean Sarah *is* ... *black*. And I am Sarah's sister so –

SARAH So she's black too. It only makes sense. I can't be black if she isn't black. Right, Eleanor.

ELEANOR Right. [*to* GAIL] And Sarah ... is ... *black*. Do you understand, Gail.

GAIL Ah ... I guess.

SARAH Well look at me. Whatya mean 'I guess.' Look at me. Isn't it obvious.

ELEANOR Yes.

SARAH I'm asking her!

[*The phone rings in the outer office*]

ELEANOR That's our phone. Would you get it for me, Sarah. Take a message.

SARAH I don't take messages. I only send messages. I can't be a receptacle. It's dangerous to my health.

ELEANOR I don't want to talk to anyone. Mr. Maxwell has been getting some very strange calls from some of his new breed of clients. Just tell whoever it is we're not available.

SARAH Strange calls? Threatening calls I bet. People threatening Petie. Okay, that I can handle.

[SARAH *rushes out*]

ELEANOR It's risky letting her answer the phone. But I had to talk to you alone.

GAIL She thinks she's black?

ELEANOR Well maybe she wants us to think she's black. Or maybe she just wants us to think she thinks she's black. It's hard to say.... Or yes maybe in her mind, truly she's black.

GAIL She's ill?

ELEANOR Yes. But she's courageous. She's always been very courageous. The doctors think she has to have a way, even in her state, to manifest her courage. That her courage is still the most important thing to her.

GAIL So she thinks it takes courage to be black.

ELEANOR Well doesn't it dear.

GAIL I don't know.... It's not like we have a choice. I mean

35

does it take courage to be what you are when there's no
way you could be anything else.

ELEANOR   That's beyond me. Sarah is beyond me too. Even when
she was well. Actually, looking back I'm not sure she
was ever well. But she was always beyond me.
[SARAH *comes on*]

SARAH   I'm back. Stop talking about me.

GAIL   We … weren't.

SARAH   Sure you were. I don't mind. Just don't do it to my face!
I took a message. I made an exception just this once. It
was someone looking for Petie. Sean Harris. Sounded
smooth. Too smooth. Talking to him almost gave me the
runs.
[SARAH *hears* MAXWELL *coming. Hides behind the couch.*
MAXWELL *comes in. Carrying two large pizza boxes*]

MAXWELL   It's a party. I've got the food. Double cheese. Double
mushrooms. Double everything.
[GAIL *gets up*]

GAIL   Did you see Dave.

MAXWELL   I saw him. He saw me. We recognized each other
immediately. We talked. He told me his story. I told him
mine. His was truly painful. But mine was much
longer.… Well, more complex. Somewhere between his
pain and my complexity we reached a common ground.
[SARAH *stands*]

SARAH   The commonality of complex pain. That makes sense.
It's the thing that ties us all together. All living things.
Regardless of race or religion.

MAXWELL   Honey. You're out.

SARAH   I escaped.

MAXWELL   [*to* ELEANOR] Is that true.

ELEANOR   She was released.

SARAH   I had myself re-diagnosed. Obsessive – compulsive. I
told them I just wanted to wash my hands all the time.
What harm can that do.
[SARAH *and* MAXWELL *are approaching each other slowly*]

MAXWELL   They bought that?

SARAH   They're in a buying mood. Space is at a premium in that
place. Anyway I think of it as an heroic escape.

MAXWELL   Well you're out. That's the only important fact. Saves me the trouble of breaking you out. I was this close to doing it too. Do you believe me.

SARAH I believe everyone.

[*They hug*]

ELEANOR [*to* MAXWELL] Tell Gail about her husband, for God's sake. Can't you see her sitting there. Can't you see how anxious she is. For God's sake, Peter.

GAIL Please!

MAXWELL He's fine. Says he's fine. He misses you.

GAIL I know he misses me. I know he says he's fine. I know all that. I didn't come to you so you could tell me things I know. How are you going to get him out of that place!

MAXWELL An appeal. A new trial.

ELEANOR Based on what.

MAXWELL New evidence.

GAIL What new evidence.

MAXWELL Things which will soon come to light.

ELEANOR What things.

MAXWELL Things which I fabricate.

ELEANOR Oh no. Come on now.

MAXWELL Brilliant fabrications. Totally supportable. Riddled with detail. An impenetrable tapestry of cast-iron bullshit.

ELEANOR You'll go to prison. You'll really help him that way. You'll find a common ground all right. You'll be playing checkers together for ten years.

SARAH You won't like prison, Petie. Prison will be death for your neo-persona. Besides everyone spits in prison. They spit everywhere. Spit stains on the walls, the floors, on all the gym equipment –

GAIL I'm getting another lawyer. I knew in my bones this was a mistake. All you've done for me is make me nervous. Make me nervous and make me write things. I've been sitting here for hours writing and trembling. I've got about a hundred pages of really shitty handwriting and all you've –

MAXWELL A hundred pages?! I'm ecstatic. Where is it. Get it.

GAIL No. I'm leaving.

MAXWELL You can't leave. I'm your only hope. That is until Eleanor here realizes her potential.

ELEANOR Leave me out of this.

37

MAXWELL [*to* GAIL] I'm sorry. I wish there was someone better. But there isn't. There's just me. Fate's cruel like that sometimes. I wish I looked better. Bigger. I wish my voice was deeper. I wish I still had all my brain. But I don't. All I have is my growth potential. And my belief. I'll get Dave out of prison though. And I'll get him out the only way there is to get him out. By undermining the system that put him there.

SARAH [*to* ELEANOR] Is Dave innocent.

MAXWELL Don't answer that, Eleanor. We don't use the word 'innocent' around here any more. The simple fact is that he's far less guilty than the two sleazy hoods that the system let go.

SARAH So you're just correcting an imbalance. I can relate to that. I love you.

MAXWELL I love you too.

SARAH [*to* ELEANOR] We love each other.

ELEANOR I'm happy for you both.

SARAH Don't get all sappy. Nothing's gonna come from it. He's only got about twenty minutes to live. And I'm incurably insane.

ELEANOR We don't use the word insane, Sarah.

SARAH I do. And I'm the expert.

MAXWELL [*to* GAIL] Please stay. Please. Show me your writing.

GAIL Why.

MAXWELL I need it. I need the whole picture. I need to put your story together with Dave's story so that I can write the epilogue. Please get it. Please trust me.

GAIL Oh, I hate this feeling. I feel like I've got no choice. Why.

MAXWELL Because you're pathetic. Don't be offended. I'm the same way. We're all pathetic. Do you feel like you've got any real choice about anything Sarah.

SARAH No.

MAXWELL Do you Eleanor.

ELEANOR Yes.

MAXWELL Yeah, well Eleanor is less pathetic than the rest of us. Good for her. We might have to use Eleanor a little later. She might be the only one left standing. [*to* GAIL] I'll get the food out. You go get your writing. Okay?

GAIL Yeah, I guess.... Okay.

[GAIL *leaves*]

38

MAXWELL Who wants pizza. I do. I do. You know I never ate pizza in my former life. It just wasn't done. Don't ask me why.

ELEANOR Why would we want to ask you why. Is it important.

MAXWELL It could be Eleanor. I don't know for sure.

SARAH Yuk. Look at that stuff. All stuck together. I'm not eating that. If you want me to eat that you've got to separate everything.

MAXWELL Sure. No problem.

ELEANOR Give me her piece. I'll do it.

[MAXWELL *hands* ELEANOR *a slice*]

SARAH Take the mushrooms off the green peppers. Take the green peppers off the tomato slices. Move them over. Move them over!

ELEANOR I'm trying!

MAXWELL Any messages?

ELEANOR Sean called.

MAXWELL What's he want.

ELEANOR Call him! Find out!

MAXWELL You're a bit testy today, Eleanor.

ELEANOR I wonder why!!

SARAH It won't work! Look. It's just all sticking together. There's a mushroom deep inside that sauce. It's the cheese. It's ruining everything. Everything's sticking to the cheese! It's gotta go. Give it to me. I'm gonna wash it. Give it to me!

[SARAH *grabs the slice*]

ELEANOR There's a washroom down the hall.

SARAH I know that! I've been here before, Eleanor.

ELEANOR I was just –

SARAH I'm not your child, Eleanor. Be careful you don't talk to me like your child. There is no gain in that attitude for either of us. [*starts off. Stops*] Anyone else want theirs washed.

MAXWELL No. I'm fine.

ELEANOR So am I.

SARAH Well suit yourself. It's gonna form a big ball in your lower intestine. It'll sit there for weeks. But it's your life.... It's your life!

[*She leaves.* ELEANOR *bends over. Puts her head in her hands*]

MAXWELL Cheer up. She seems much better.

39

ELEANOR Be quiet. [*looks up*] What would you know about it.

MAXWELL All those times I've visited her in the hospital these last few months. We've talked. We've looked into each other's souls. We have this uncanny communication. We don't always use words. Sometimes we just look at each other and nod ... slowly. Very slow nodding. Like this.... [*he demonstrates*] It's amazing.

ELEANOR You're worse than she is.

MAXWELL You think so? Well I don't feel so bad. So that should be good news to you. I mean in relative terms –

ELEANOR Be quiet! Call Sean. Do some business. Act like a professional lawyer please. Just once or twice a day. Please. Call Sean!

MAXWELL I'll get right on it.

[*MAXWELL picks up the phone. Dials.* GAIL *comes back in. Carrying three large legal-size yellow pads*]

GAIL I think a lot of it's illegible. Especially the really personal parts. And there are tear stains. [*to* ELEANOR] Do you believe it. I cried like a baby a few times. It was awful.

MAXWELL Sounds terrific, honey. I'll be right with you.

GAIL [*to* ELEANOR] What's he doing.

ELEANOR Calling his ex-partner.

GAIL About Dave?

ELEANOR I don't think so. [*to* MAXWELL] Is it about Dave, Peter.

MAXWELL Dave who?

GAIL Oh shit. [*sits*]

MAXWELL Hello. Sean Harris please.... Yeah, it's Peter – Petie Maxwell. [*to* GAIL] I'll be right with you honey. Relax.... [*to* ELEANOR] Gee look at all those pages.... Looks great.... Hi Sean.... Yeah.... No.... No I haven't.... No.... That's right no. Yes.... Yes.... Yes! Oh. Good for you.... Good for him too.... Oh, really. What was that.... Say that again. Come on say it again. I just want to make sure I get it on tape. Yeah that's right.... I am. I'm taping you. Well.... What ... ? The same to you I guess! [*he hangs up*] That man is turning into a psychopath. He threatened my life.

ELEANOR He didn't.

MAXWELL I've got it on tape.

ELEANOR No you don't.

MAXWELL Oh right. That was a bluff. I've got to be careful. I'm

starting to believe in my own fantasies. Mostly I think
that's a good thing, but there are times we have to be
careful not to –

ELEANOR Be quiet. What was it about. Conner?

MAXWELL Yeah. The same things. But more desperate. 'Babe
Conner's an important man. A powerful man.
Untouchable.'

[GAIL *starts flipping through her pad madly*]

ELEANOR Well that's true. You know that. How can you fight him if
you won't even acknowledge a simple truth about him.

MAXWELL It's an implied truth. It's the implication that I'm
fighting.

ELEANOR Yes but –

GAIL What was that name.

ELEANOR What name, dear.

GAIL The name he said just now. The powerful man's name.

MAXWELL Conner.

GAIL The first name.

ELEANOR John.

GAIL No he didn't say John. What was it.

MAXWELL Babe.

[*He is walking toward* GAIL]

GAIL Yeah. Babe.... Some guy ... called Babe.... Some rich guy.
Dave said those hoods were probably working for
someone who – Here it is!

MAXWELL Let me see that.

[*He grabs the pad from* GAIL. *Starts to read*]

GAIL Who is he.

ELEANOR [*stands*] Come on now. Let's be careful here.

GAIL Who is he. Who is he!

[MAXWELL *looks up*]

MAXWELL He's dead meat! He's the end of an era. He's ... your
husband's ticket out of prison.

[GAIL *stands*]

GAIL Really? You think so? How.

MAXWELL These things in here. These things you wrote. Are they
true.

GAIL I don't know. What things. What I wrote about Dave and
me ... our life together. That's true.

MAXWELL These things the hoods said about the rich guy.

GAIL They told Dave they've been doing crooked things for

41

him for years. I don't know if that's true or not. Neither
did Dave.

MAXWELL Well why wouldn't it be true.

ELEANOR I can't believe a man with your experience in criminal
law is asking that question. Examine the source.

MAXWELL You think crooks can't tell the truth? Crooks can lie.
Crooks can tell the truth. Everyone get their coats.

ELEANOR Why.

MAXWELL We've got work to do. We've each got an assignment.
We're spreading out. Get your coats.
[GAIL *leaves*]

ELEANOR What assignment. Spreading out where.

MAXWELL It's a mission in search of the relative truth. I'll explain
on the way out.
[*He throws Gail's pads on the desk*]

ELEANOR I can't leave. What about Sarah.

MAXWELL Sarah's fine. You're not her mother.

ELEANOR Don't you start!

MAXWELL You'll have to leave her alone sometime. You can't glue
yourself to her. Do both of you a favour. Trust her. She is
what she is. She'll do what she has to do.

ELEANOR Easy for you. You're not responsible for her. I'm her legal
guardian.

MAXWELL So what! Big deal! Who gives a shit about that stuff
anymore! It's linear. Legal guardian is a linear concept!
Try being her sister. Come on. I need you.
[*He tries to push her out the door*]

ELEANOR Let me just tell her we're leaving.

MAXWELL No. She'll want to come with us. It's too dangerous.

ELEANOR Wait a minute now! Who says danger is part of my job.
I'm a legal secretary.

MAXWELL No! How can you be a legal secretary! Not now. That's
part of the linear past too. Think about it. We're just
friends. Friends in the struggle. Okay, okay. You just go
to the library for now. We'll include you in the
dangerous part later.

ELEANOR God help us all.

MAXWELL Sure. If she has the time.
[*They are gone*]
[*Blackout*]

Scene Four

Two hours later
> SARAH *is sitting behind Maxwell's desk. Feet up.*
Reading Gail's story. Crying gently. Humming an African song
> *A knock on the outer door. Sound of it opening*
> *Muffled voices*
> HARRIS *and* CONNER *come in. Overcoats, silk scarves.*
Look at SARAH. *At each other*

HARRIS Excuse me?... Excuse me?

SARAH Be with you in a minute. Just want to finish reading this beautiful paragraph.... Beautiful and sad. This girl's a genius. Someone should tell her.... I'll do it.
> [SARAH *looks up*]

HARRIS We're looking for Peter Maxwell.

SARAH Not here.

CONNER Yeah, we can see that. Is he coming back.

SARAH Sure.

CONNER When.

SARAH Don't know.

HARRIS Are you a friend of his.
> [*She looks at them for a moment*]

SARAH Are you.

CONNER [*to* HARRIS] Fuck him. Let's go.

HARRIS I think it's worth one final effort all things considered. Don't you.

CONNER Yeah. I guess.

HARRIS [*to* SARAH] Do you mind if we wait.

SARAH Sure. Wait. Sit on that couch.

HARRIS Thanks. We know it's late. But we saw the lights on. I heard he works late. Sometimes even sleeps here.
> [*They take off their coats. They both have on black and white formal wear.* SARAH *bolts out of her chair*]

SARAH Holy shit! You look like a couple of vampires!... You can't walk around with those things on. Don't you realize the images those things conjure up.

HARRIS We've just come from a function.

SARAH You look like you've come from a dinner at the

43

Reichstag. Some family affair of the Third Reich. You look like Goering. You look like Speer.

CONNER [*to* HARRIS] What is all this Nazi crap around here. Are these people living in the goddamn past.... I mean, it's starting to really annoy me.

SARAH Take them off. Take them off!... Come on. They're scaring me. I'm gonna wet my pants or something. Jesus. At least loosen the ties. Undo a button or two. You look like machines. Nazi vampire machines. I'm getting scared. Look guys I really mean it.... Loosen your ties!!
[HARRIS *does*]

HARRIS [*to* CONNER *in a whisper*] Loosen your tie.

CONNER What for.

HARRIS She's scared. Look at her.

CONNER That's her problem. It's a tie. It's just a tie.

HARRIS So just loosen it. What's the big deal. It scares her.

CONNER Why.

HARRIS I don't know. Ask her.

CONNER Ah. The hell with it. [*he loosens his tie*]

HARRIS [*to* SARAH] Better?

SARAH A little.... So you were at a function. That's nice. I used to function.... Now I just dream. [*she starts to read again*]

CONNER What's she talking about.

HARRIS I don't know.

CONNER Who is she.

HARRIS I don't know.

CONNER Ask her.

HARRIS You ask her.

CONNER [*to* SARAH] Hey you! What are you doing here. Are you a client.
[SARAH *looks up. Slowly*]

SARAH Client? What made you ask that. Why didn't you ask if I was a lawyer. Does it look like I couldn't be a lawyer ... for some reason.

HARRIS Are you a lawyer.

SARAH Yes.

HARRIS You work with Mr. Maxwell?

SARAH I'm his new partner. My name is Sarah Downey.
[*She stands, walks to them. Puts out her hand.* HARRIS *and* CONNER *look at each other. Shake with her in turn*]

HARRIS Sean Harris.

CONNER John ... Conner.

SARAH Perhaps I can help you. Are you looking for a lawyer.

CONNER We're looking for Maxwell.

SARAH You have ... some reason you don't want to do business with me.... You don't do business with black people?

HARRIS I beg your pardon.

SARAH Oh excuse me. I should have been more subtle. But sometimes the yoke slips you know. The beast escapes. Stands up straight. Tells it like it is.

[*She gives them a Nazi salute*]

CONNER Let's get outta here.

HARRIS Okay.

SARAH Okay?... Okay okay. I've had my laugh. You guys are too much. Lighten up! I'm sorry for stringing you along. I don't know. Maybe it's the way you're dressed. It just brought out the mischief in me. You gotta believe me. I'm sorry. Now what can I do for you.... Come on. I'm Peter's partner. Do you want to see my degree?

[*And now* SARAH *is a lawyer. A pretty good one*]

CONNER & HARRIS Yes.

SARAH What is it. The way I'm dressed? I was cleaning up the office. We can't afford a janitor for God's sake. Come on what's the problem. You have some problem with Peter, I take it.... Something I can probably help you with.

CONNER I want him off my back. You think you can arrange that?

SARAH You're going to have to fill me in here. Peter isn't exactly the most professional of individuals these days. It's his illness, you know. The communication around this office isn't what it should be. He's harassing you. Is that what you're implying.

CONNER Yeah he's –

HARRIS I think it's better if we wait for Mr. Maxwell.

SARAH Okay. But I'm telling you you won't get anywhere with him. He's not behaving rationally.

CONNER You've noticed that, eh.

SARAH Well it's hard not to. Come on. Seriously. You can level with me. I was just kidding before. It's late. It's been a hard day. I spent most of it covering up for Peter's lack of judgement.

[CONNER *takes* HARRIS *aside*]

CONNER Obviously she's got a lot in common with the guy. Obviously she knows the guy. She's got a bead on him. Maybe we *can* work this out with her. [*to* SARAH] I'm offering the hand of peace. That's basically what I'm doing. You know me, don't you. You recognize me, I know you do.

HARRIS Maybe she doesn't.

CONNER Everybody in this city recognizes me. She lives in this city doesn't she.

HARRIS Maybe she doesn't.

SARAH [*to* HARRIS] Whatya mean by that.

HARRIS Nothing. Maybe you're from out of town.... You know from some other place.

SARAH I used to be from some other place. I'm from here now. I mean I'm trying my best. Come on, give me a chance. I recognize him. He's famous.

CONNER I wouldn't say famous. I get around though. I make my contributions.

HARRIS Mr. Conner is the publisher of *The World Today.*

CONNER She knows that.

SARAH Yeah I know that.... That's the paper with all the colour. Lots of blue and red. I like that paper.

CONNER You do?

SARAH I like it a lot. I read it. I like the way all the articles are surrounded by colour. Borders, I mean. Colourful borders. And the writers, they're interesting. They're mad. They all write like they're really ticked off. I like their angry attitude. I can relate to it.

CONNER Do you subscribe.

SARAH To what.

CONNER To what? The paper.

SARAH No. I like it though. I read it on subways. I pick it off the floor. I read it carefully. Then I put it back on the floor before I get off.

CONNER People in general like my paper. It gives them what they need. It has balls.

SARAH I like balls. Maybe that's why I like your paper. Not the colour at all. The balls.

CONNER Yeah.

SARAH And a cock.

46

CONNER What.

SARAH A cock. Your paper's got a cock. A big cock. That's good. I mean let's stop pretending it doesn't matter.... I know it matters to me. I bet it matters to you too.

CONNER Well yeah ... it –

SARAH I'm talking about the paper now.

CONNER Yeah.... So am I.... I mean –

SARAH I like the positions it takes on all the tough issues.

CONNER Those are my positions.

SARAH I like your positions.... Some people don't. But I do. Your position on downtown development.

CONNER I'm for it.

SARAH Who isn't for it. Assholes aren't for it. Do I look like an asshole.

CONNER No you don't. You look unconventional. You act unconventional. But that doesn't make you an asshole.

SARAH No more than that outfit makes you an asshole. Remember I was just kidding you before.

CONNER I knew that.

SARAH Your position on downtown development is closely tied to your position on public housing. Would that be an accurate observation.

CONNER I think so. Yes.... Wealth leads to wealth. Keep the downtown growing. Eventually there'll be so much money in this city there won't be any need for public housing.

SARAH Amen to that.... Halfway houses?

CONNER Pardon.

SARAH Halfway houses for released prisoners. Mental patients.

CONNER Now that's a problem.

SARAH You got a solution?

CONNER I think I do, ah.... [*he snaps his fingers*]

SARAH Sarah.

CONNER I think I do, Sarah. I think I've got a solution. I believe we have to protect the vast –

SARAH No don't tell me. It's probably too complex. I mean there's only so much I can handle at one time. That is unless it's a simple solution. Something real simple. Like killing them.

CONNER Killing who.

SARAH The released prisoners. The mental patients. That would work.

CONNER Sure it would work. But it's not going to happen.

HARRIS Babe.

CONNER I mean I don't want it to happen.

SARAH Me neither. But it would be a simple solution.

HARRIS Mr. Conner doesn't believe in simple solutions.

CONNER What are you saying Sean. My whole career is based on offering up simple solutions.

HARRIS Yes. But not *that* simple. Not solutions like *that*.

CONNER Of course not. She knows that.

SARAH I was just speculating. Now there's a much maligned word.... Speculation!

CONNER Oh, God almighty. You're telling me. The whole bloody country is based on speculation. The entire goddamn economy. Everything we eat, we wear, we use. But you hear these people talk about it like it was a mortal sin. These people need a fucking fist down their....
[HARRIS *grabs* CONNER's *shoulder. Squeezes*]

SARAH By 'these people,' I assume you mean people like Mr. Maxwell.

CONNER He's your partner. I won't say anything bad about him ... to your face.
[CONNER *laughs.* SARAH *laughs*]

SARAH Yes that would be awkward. Especially when he has so little time left.

HARRIS What do you mean.

SARAH A year. Maybe less.

HARRIS Are you sure.

SARAH You seem concerned. Why is that.

CONNER Sean used to be his partner.

SARAH Of course. He's mentioned you. I remember now.

CONNER What's he say about him.

SARAH He says he works for disgusting criminals.

CONNER [*laughs*] He works for me!

SARAH [*laughs*] He knows that!

CONNER Damn that man. That man is misrepresenting me in a very public way. I'm a public man and he's attacking me in a very distressing and personal manner. He doesn't know me. Know what I came from. I came from nowhere. I wasn't born connected like Sean here. I built my connections. I started as a shipper.

HARRIS She doesn't want to hear your life story.

SARAH I don't mind. [*to* CONNER] Is it a good story. Is it like your paper. Is it angry. Does it have lots of colour.

CONNER I was born into a working-class family. My father was a streetcar driver. My mother –

HARRIS Look, John. None of that's important at the moment.

CONNER I was just trying to let her know how hard I –

SARAH I'm afraid he's right, John. As fascinating as it sounds, it'll have to wait. We've got a problem with Mr. Maxwell that's in desperate need of a simple solution.

HARRIS Do you have influence with Peter. Can you persuade him, in your own way, to stop his attack on my client here.

SARAH I can try.

HARRIS Well that would be good. Because you see Miss –

SARAH Ms.

HARRIS Ms ... ah ... Sarah.... We could all benefit from a reasonable intervention –

SARAH Look. No need to say more. I know where you're coming from. You're reasonable men. You want a reasonably simple solution. I'll talk to Peter. Whatever he's doing, he's doing it because he's dying. It makes some people bitter. There's no way around that.

CONNER We could cause him a lot of trouble. If he's dying, he doesn't need any more trouble, does he.

SARAH Well put. Simply put. Very simply put. Just leave it with me. I'll have my girl call you. Keep you posted.

HARRIS We could stay. Maybe we should stay and reinforce your arguments.

CONNER We could do that for you, Sarah.

SARAH He's a weak old man. I can twist him around my finger.

CONNER He just hates me. He hates me for reasons I don't understand. It's awful.

SARAH He's dying Mr. Conner. And you're not. You're in your prime. You've got everything. He's got nothing. Wait a minute. Maybe that's the answer. Give him something.

CONNER What.

SARAH Money.

HARRIS I don't think that's advisable.

SARAH Not in a cheque. Nothing that could be traced. Nothing he could use against you. Cash.

CONNER How much cash.

SARAH How much you got?

[CONNER *takes out his wallet*]

HARRIS My advice on this Babe, would be that –

CONNER She knows the guy. Maybe she's right. Maybe we've blown it out of proportion. Maybe it's just envy. [*to* SARAH] I've got twenty-seven hundred dollars.

SARAH Good. That's good. That's a lot to someone like Petie.

HARRIS He used to spend that much on a raincoat. This won't work.

CONNER It might. Maybe he regrets giving up everything he owns. It's scary down here in the bowels of hell without any resources.

SARAH It's worth a try. Especially when you consider his alternatives. What are his alternatives ... I mean, as you see them? [*she takes the money*]

HARRIS Unpleasant.

CONNER Yeah. Very unpleasant.

SARAH Hey. Don't get me wrong now, guys. But that sounds like a threat.

[GAIL *comes on*]

GAIL Hi.

SARAH [*to* CONNER] Be with you in a moment.

[SARAH *goes to* GAIL]

GAIL Where is he.

SARAH [*whispering*] I loved your book by the way. I laughed, I cried. Be with you in a moment. Now where was I. Oh yeah, I was getting money. Petie says to always get money from them. I'll be with you in a moment.

[SARAH *rushes back to* CONNER *and* HARRIS]

SARAH How much have you got Mr. Harris!

HARRIS Me? This isn't my battle.

SARAH It's a loan. [*to* CONNER] Isn't it. [*to* HARRIS] Your client will pay you back. [*to* CONNER] Won't you.

CONNER Sure. No problem. Give her some money.

HARRIS I don't carry cash.

SARAH I'll take your coat. And your shoes! And your silky silky scarf!! Hand them over. Do it now!

HARRIS What are you talking about.

SARAH Careful now. I've got a witness now. [*to* GAIL] Oh Gail, thank God you're here. They had me backed against a wall. I was terrified. Well look at them. They're terrifying. I think they're with the secret police. Smell them. It's the smell of rancid fascist slime.

CONNER Hey, you're starting up again. I thought you were a reasonable person.

[*He grabs the money from her*]

SARAH Well that just shows how stupid you are. I'm a mental patient. You've been tricked by a person with a shattered mind. Someone who should just be put out of her misery. I was just playing for time. Waiting for reinforcements. They're here now. Aren't you Gail.

GAIL Yeah. I guess.

SARAH These guys are after Petie. They're hatching vile plots against him.

[CONNER *grabs* HARRIS]

CONNER Look, you're my lawyer and I want some answers from you right now! Who is this person and what the hell is she talking about. At first I thought she was wacky. Then she seemed okay. Now she's wacky again. If I had to bet, I'd bet she really is a mental patient. I'm confused by this, so what are you going to do about it.

HARRIS I think we should leave, Babe.

CONNER Good.

[*They start off*]

GAIL He called him Babe. Babe's the name of the guy who got Dave sent to prison.

[GAIL *is blocking their way to the door*]

HARRIS [*to* CONNER] Who's Dave.

CONNER How the fuck should I know.

GAIL He's my husband. And your goons set him up.

SARAH That right, Babe?

CONNER I don't know what the hell she's talking about.

GAIL Mr. Maxwell has proof.

HARRIS What proof.

[HARRIS *and* CONNER *advance*]

SARAH She's not saying.

[SARAH *grabs* GAIL. *Pushes her out of the way*]

GAIL Yeah. That's right. I'm not.

CONNER Oh you'll say all right.
        [*He starts to advance on* GAIL]
HARRIS   [*grabs* CONNER's *arm*] Babe. Don't.
        [CONNER *throws* HARRIS *off.* HARRIS *falls back onto the
        couch.* CONNER *is still advancing on* GAIL]
CONNER I've taken just about enough shit from you people....
        Now what proof are you talking about.
        [GAIL *is backing up*]
SARAH   Stay away from her.
        [SARAH *grabs him. He tosses her off. She lands on* HARRIS]
CONNER Eat shit you crazy bitch. [*to* GAIL] Now what's going on
        here. Is this a shakedown. Who are you working for.
        [CONNER *is chasing* GAIL *around the desk.* HARRIS *and*
        SARAH *are struggling on the couch*]
GAIL   We did nothing to you. We were just minding our own
        business. Your two punks threatened my life. A guy
        named Moore. A guy named Dawson.
CONNER You've got something connecting me to those men?
        What is it. [*suddenly he reaches over the desk and grabs
        her hair*] What is it!?
        [*She bites his hand. He yells. Grabs her in a head lock.
        Somehow* SARAH *is on* HARRIS' *shoulder. Pulling his hair.
        He is stumbling toward* GAIL *and* CONNER. SARAH *yells.
        Goes from* HARRIS' *shoulders to* CONNER's *back. They start
        to spin. All four of them with* HARRIS *holding on. After a
        few spins,* HARRIS *is thrown off balance. Falls against the
        wall. Hitting the switch to the conveyor belt. Turning it
        on.* HARRIS *falls on the conveyor belt, gets his coat stuck.
        And is going up the conveyor belt, as he yells at the
        others*]
HARRIS   Please! Come on now. Babe, this is something we don't
        need. Ladies. Please. This is a misunderstanding. We
        can work this out. We can do better than this!
        [SARAH, GAIL, *and* CONNER *are a mass of punching, kicking,
        groaning bodies on the floor by now*]
        Please!
        [*Blackout*]
        [*INTERMISSION*]

52

Scene Five

Just a few minutes later
 The office is a mess. Papers everywhere. A filing cabinet overturned
 GAIL *is sitting on the floor against the desk.* SARAH *is lying face down near the door*

GAIL Are you all right.
 [SARAH *raises her fist*]
 I was scared. I was angry. But I was scared too. I think he wanted to kill us. I'm still shaking.

SARAH [*sitting*] I feel good. I got in a few really good whacks. I liked it when I hit him in the nose. I liked the sound. A kind of whomp. Then a kind of whoosh. Whomp. Woosh. Whompwoosh. It was satisfying. Maybe I should have started hitting earlier in my life. [*stands*] Honestly. I feel great. I think I might have a broken rib though.

GAIL Seriously?
 [SARAH *gets on her knees. Crawls over to* GAIL]

SARAH It'll heal. It's a bone. Bones heal.

GAIL Maybe we should take you to a hospital.

SARAH Hospital? No thank you. I usually have a hell of a time getting out once I'm in.

GAIL I've never been in a fight with a guy in a tuxedo before. It was interesting because of that. And he had a lot of cologne on too. Rolling around like that. Ripping away at all that expensive material. Smelling that expensive cologne close up. It was interesting and weird.

SARAH My father smelled good. He smelled 'new.' Always. And he had a lot of nice clothes.

GAIL Was he rich.

SARAH Yeah. And white.
 [*Pause*]

GAIL Was your mother white.

SARAH Oh yes. She was whiter than my father. She was one of the whitest people on the planet. She was famous in certain circles for it.

GAIL So ... just you and Eleanor are ... black.

SARAH Eleanor's not black.... Not really.

53

GAIL Oh.
       [*Pause*]
SARAH Me neither. Not really....
GAIL You just pretend to be black sometimes. Is that right.
SARAH It helps me get angry. It makes me feel brave.
GAIL You are brave.
SARAH No. I'm crazy.... You know ... unrealistic.
       [SARAH *points to her own head. Shakes it. Sadly*]
GAIL You attacked that guy because I was in trouble. That guy
       is big. And mean.
SARAH And in some way crazier than me. I could sense it. He's
       hearing voices. His voices are ugly. And very confident. I
       felt a connection to the guy. It wasn't a nice feeling.
GAIL I felt a rage. I guess that's normal. What he did to Dave.
       And he's rich. It's normal to feel that about the rich, I
       guess. My family does. I don't though. Not usually.
       Usually I don't care. The rich have got their lives. I've got
       mine. Theirs are better in some ways. Mine's better in
       other ways. Maybe it evens out. Or maybe it doesn't.
       Maybe I'm just kidding myself. Maybe that's why I felt
       the rage. Confusing, isn't it.
SARAH No. I understand. But that doesn't mean much. Usually
       the only person I understand is myself. And I don't
       make any sense.
GAIL You're making sense now.
SARAH Did I take a pill. I don't remember. [*she takes a small
       bottle from her pocket*] Did you see me take one of
       these.
GAIL No.
       [*Another bottle*]
SARAH Or these?
GAIL No.
       [*Another bottle*]
SARAH Or these?
GAIL No.
SARAH [*stands*] Really. Must have been the fight. It must have
       been therapeutic. Jesus. Wait till I tell my doctor. 'I don't
       need the drugs anymore, doc. I just need a good
       punch-up every once in awhile.' Maybe he'll let me beat
       up on him. I'd like to. He says he cares. He's supposed

to be so dedicated. Maybe he'd let me kick him in the face once a week. Punch his teeth out. Rip his fucking balls off! [*pause*] Sorry.

GAIL That's okay.

[*Pause*]

SARAH I liked your book!

GAIL What book.

SARAH Your story. I read the proofs.... Where is it by the way. I put it on the desk.

[GAIL *gets up. Starts to look for it*]

I used to read a lot. I used to know people in publishing. I think I used to be in publishing. Can't remember exactly what I did but it was something fairly important.

[GAIL *finds the pad on the floor behind the desk. Picks it up*]

GAIL It's not a book. It's not a story.

SARAH No trust me. I know about these things for some reason. It's great. You write great. It took me away.

GAIL I was just writing it for Mr. Maxwell. It's supposed to help him with Dave's case.

SARAH It's transcendental. It's gone beyond its initial and common purpose. It's living in the area of a new possibility. It'll make people giddy with sadness. You have to get it published.

GAIL No. It's private. It's my life. I don't think I'd want a lot of strangers reading it.

[ELEANOR *and* MAXWELL *come on.* ELEANOR *is supporting* MAXWELL. *He has his arm over her shoulder*]

ELEANOR Help me. Please.

[GAIL *goes to them.* SARAH *sees* MAXWELL. *Gets scared. Goes into a corner*]

GAIL What's wrong with him.

ELEANOR I found him collapsed on the steps outside. I think he's having a relapse.

MAXWELL I'm fine. I just lost my breath.

ELEANOR Good God! What happened here. Did you do this Sarah. [*to* GAIL] Did she do this.

GAIL I'll explain later.... Why don't we put him on the couch.

MAXWELL Good plan. A little rest. A little sleep. Even if I slip into a coma for awhile, that's not necessarily a bad thing.

ELEANOR I'm calling an ambulance.

MAXWELL No. Please don't. It's not serious.

ELEANOR Be quiet. You don't know if it's serious or not.

MAXWELL I think ... I just ... hypervent – [*he stumbles. Falls onto the couch*]

ELEANOR Enough is enough. I let you move us into this pathetic little hole against my better judgement. But I'm not going to let you die here. [*she goes to the desk*] Where's the phone.

SARAH Doesn't matter. It's broken.

GAIL It got broken in the fight....

ELEANOR You two had a fight? Did she attack you.

SARAH That's your worst fear isn't it Eleanor. When have I ever been violent. Never. [*to* GAIL] Never done a violent thing. But it's her worst fear.

GAIL She saved me. We were attacked.

ELEANOR Oh my God. [*to* MAXWELL] Did you hear that. That's what happens when you bring us down to this part of the city – we get attacked! Doped-up strangers break in and attack!

SARAH Do you think you should be yelling at him at this particular moment, Eleanor.

ELEANOR Yes!! I'm sorry. But yes! I can't function in this environment! Look at this place. Look at all of you. This place makes me very uneasy. You people make me very uneasy. You people all have problems. They're not my problems. I've got my own.

SARAH [*to* GAIL] She means me.

ELEANOR I don't mean you! Yes! Yes I do mean you. You're scaring me to death. You've been scaring me to death for years. [*sits down*] Why don't you just stop it. [*lowers her head*] [MAXWELL *suddenly sits up*]

MAXWELL I'm better now! I just hyperventilated. I was so excited by what I found out I just lost control. I started to run. I started to sing. Someone go get Eleanor a glass of water.

SARAH I'll go.

[SARAH *leaves*]

MAXWELL What a mess. Who were they. Did they hurt you.

GAIL We're fine.

MAXWELL Looks like you put up quite a fight. You're a tough little cookie aren't you.

56

GAIL Not really.

MAXWELL Of course you are. Who were they.

GAIL That man named 'Babe' was one. Sarah said the other one was his lawyer.

MAXWELL Dear dear dear dear dear.

ELEANOR [*lifts her head*] Sean Harris? Sean Harris attacked you?

GAIL No. The other one. You see, things got a bit out of control.

[SARAH *comes in with a glass of water*]

SARAH Yeah. Things just escalated. There was tension in the air. The situation was not healthy. Eventually the situation – escalated. Happens all the time. [*hands* ELEANOR *the water*] Do you want one of my pills, Eleanor. One won't hurt. Here. Decide later when no one's watching.

[ELEANOR *takes the bottle. Puts it on the desk*]

GAIL It all started because I told Babe we had proof he was connected to those hoods. I don't know why. I was angry. I know we don't have any proof.

MAXWELL Yes. We do. We have proof coming out the whazoo. Tons of it.

GAIL Where'd you get it.

ELEANOR He went for a long walk and made it up.

MAXWELL No. I was willing to do that. I was capable of taking that route. But I decided to do some legitimate investigation first. Usually I disdain investigation. It gives due process a respect it doesn't deserve. But, well the truth is I wanted to know if I was still mentally capable of following one piece of information logically to another and making reasonable deductions along the way.

SARAH What's that like. It sounds boring.

MAXWELL Well it's like a strong narrative in a book. It can be pleasant enough. But it's not really necessary if –

GAIL So what have you got?

MAXWELL Pictures. Would you believe it. Lovely little pictures. You see, the bad guys like to have their pictures taken with big shots. They keep scrap albums apparently. The big shots don't know about it. But it goes on. Apparently it's a real underworld trend. Life is just great when it surprises you like this.

GAIL So you've got pictures of Babe Conner with the hoods, is that right.

MAXWELL Yes it is.

ELEANOR Can I see them.

MAXWELL Sure.

[*He reaches into his pocket. Takes out a large envelope. Hands it to her.* ELEANOR *looks inside the envelope*]

ELEANOR Where did you get these.

MAXWELL I bought them.

ELEANOR You bought them?

MAXWELL Yes! I went undercover. I followed information. I found a source. I made a purchase. Two hundred dollars and worth a million times that.

ELEANOR Where did you get two hundred dollars. You don't have any money. Neither of us has any money. We're working for free these days, remember!

MAXWELL Well, I don't know how I got it. I just reached in my pocket and it was there. It was a spiritual moment. I almost swooned.

GAIL So what do we do now.

MAXWELL Well now we explore our options. There are several.

ELEANOR Here's one I think might be appropriate. Call the police.

MAXWELL I'm sorry. I'd like to. Just for your sake Eleanor if for no other reason. I know you still have a reservoir of faith in the veneer of civilization. But I can't. The police are encumbered by their role within the system. The system is the thing which caused the turmoil in the first place.

SARAH What's he talking about. I love what he's saying. But what does it have to do with anything I could do.

GAIL He's talking about getting Dave out of prison.

ELEANOR No he's not.

[GAIL *throws her hands up in the air*]

MAXWELL You're right. Dave's just part of it. What we have here is a focal point in the struggle. An historical watershed. A convergence of apparently random injustices. And it is our duty – *our* duty – to take this moment and amplify its significance until it reverberates to a point where the walls come tumbling down. The walls which surround the privileged and the self-righteous, the walls which ... which – [*he grabs his head*] Oooh that's a bit scary.... I'll be honest now.... It's pain.

[ELEANOR *grabs his arm*]

ELEANOR Okay, that's it! You're going to a hospital.
[MAXWELL *falls to the floor*]

MAXWELL No. When the time comes … I want to skip the hospital and go directly to the morgue.

SARAH I can relate to that. Get rid of the middleman.

ELEANOR Hyperventilation. You were lying. Admit it.
[ELEANOR *is trying to pick him up*]

MAXWELL I was just thinking positively.

ELEANOR You're having another stroke. I can't allow you to die here.

MAXWELL I want to die here.
[MAXWELL *frees himself from* ELEANOR]

SARAH [*looking scared*] He wants to *die* here.
[SARAH *goes into a corner*]

MAXWELL I don't mean to be rude but it *is* my death after all. And I'd rather go through it without tubes and wires.

ELEANOR [*looks at* SARAH *and* GAIL] Isn't anyone going to help me convince him.

SARAH Don't look at me. I don't get that 'will-to-live' stuff in the first place. I'd like to inject us all with enough pure heroin to put us permanently out of our misery within minutes….That's a lie.

GAIL I think he's right, Eleanor. My father died in the hospital. They kept him alive with all those things. It didn't make anyone very happy. He wasn't happy. My mother wasn't happy either.
[MAXWELL *is rocking back and forth. Holding his head.* SARAH *turns toward them tentatively*]

SARAH Besides, maybe he's all right. Why don't we just think of him as being all right. You know, just think him back to health.

MAXWELL Yeah. That's a plan I like. Oooh. Pain pain pain.

ELEANOR It's not working, is it.

SARAH I haven't started yet. Let's have a little faith here Eleanor.

ELEANOR Do you think I want him to suffer. Don't you think I care. I've worked for this man for fifteen years.

GAIL Try it Eleanor. What have you got to lose. Just concentrate. Think about him being all right…. Tell yourself he's doing just fine.

SARAH Yeah. It's that easy. Concentrate.

59

[*And* SARAH *closes her eyes. Concentrates. Hard*]

MAXWELL   I think … they may be on to something here.

ELEANOR   Who are you people. How did you find one another.
Were you given maps at birth. Did God bring you
together. Do you share some mysterious ailment.

MAXWELL   I think it's working.

ELEANOR   Is it a virus.

SARAH   I think he looks better.

ELEANOR   Why am I immune.

MAXWELL   It's definitely working.

GAIL   He's definitely better. It's amazing. It's exciting too.

MAXWELL   I think I'm going to be all right.

GAIL   Sarah. Look at him. He's better. It worked.

SARAH   No thanks to any of you. I said concentrate, not talk. I
was stranded out there on the primal plane all alone.
Petie, did you feel me zapping you with those positive
negative ions.

MAXWELL   I think so.

ELEANOR   Honestly now Peter, how do you feel. Don't pretend just
to humour her.

SARAH   Oh right! The guy's going to fake recovery from brain
implosion just so he won't hurt my feelings. And she
thinks I've got a problem with reality.

MAXWELL   I'm going to stand. Aren't I, Sarah.

SARAH   Yes!

[SARAH *gets behind him. Helps him stand*]

MAXWELL   I'm standing up! I'm going to walk. Aren't I, Sarah.

SARAH   Yes!

[SARAH *starts walking with* MAXWELL. *Holding him up from
behind*]

MAXWELL   I'm walking!

SARAH   There was a time when this sort of thing would have
been considered a miracle. Not that I want the publicity,
but shouldn't we call someone.

MAXWELL   Let's see how long it lasts first.

ELEANOR   Is the pain gone.

MAXWELL   We won't use the word pain anymore. Let's forget about
pain for the time being. Okay everyone? Now we've got
to get moving here. There seems to be something about
the dynamic of this particular group that keeps us from

focusing properly. But we've got to overcome that. Time is a precious commodity. Okay ... Gail.

GAIL Yes, Mr. Maxwell.

MAXWELL Did you see Dave today.

GAIL Yes I did.

MAXWELL And he gave you the names of those two guys.

GAIL Yes. And where they live.

MAXWELL God that's good news. News like that can make a man live forever. [*he breathes in and out a few times*] Man I feel great. Really great. Okay. Eleanor.

ELEANOR Yes Peter.

MAXWELL Did you get all that stuff on Babe Conner from the library.

ELEANOR Everything they had.

MAXWELL Which was plenty.

ELEANOR Yes.

MAXWELL Yes. Because he's a high profile man. A contributor. An investor in the future. But I've looked through the hole in my head and seen his idea of the future. It's a nasty stupid place. Okay! We've got to swing into action. Gail and Sarah come with me. Eleanor, you stay here.

ELEANOR And do what.

SARAH Tidy up. [*to* MAXWELL] She loves to tidy up. She's brilliant at it. Gets it from our mother.

ELEANOR And what will the rest of you be doing if you don't mind me asking.

MAXWELL Changing the world. Our little part of it. Don't feel left out though. It's a big job. We'll need all the help we can get. You'll be included.

ELEANOR I'm grateful. Honestly.

MAXWELL Can we take your car, Eleanor.

ELEANOR Oh certainly. I'd be honoured. The keys are on my desk. [GAIL *and* SARAH *are helping* MAXWELL *to the door. He has an arm over each of their shoulders*]

SARAH This is an adventure isn't it. We're going somewhere. To do something. That's an adventure.

MAXWELL Yes it is.

GAIL Is it dangerous.

MAXWELL Yes it is. But don't worry. You'll do fine. You're a tough little cookie.

GAIL Not really.

ELEANOR Sarah stays.

SARAH Sarah goes.

[SARAH *leaves*]

ELEANOR Peter ... Peter ... Peter!

GAIL [*to* MAXWELL] We'll wait for you in the car.

[GAIL *leaves*]

[*Pause*]

[MAXWELL *is leaning against the frame of the door for support. He looks at* ELEANOR]

MAXWELL Don't be mad at me. It's just a little adventure. I mean I've got to do something to keep their spirits up. We should dedicate our new lives to people like Sarah and Gail. The troubled and marginal. You know ... those people.

ELEANOR 'Those people' trust you, Peter.

MAXWELL I know. And I'm sincerely moved by that. Their trust gives me strength.

[ELEANOR *holds up the envelope*]

ELEANOR These are fake. You had these pictures of Mr. Conner with the two criminals made up. They're fakes. And they're not even good ones.

MAXWELL They can be improved. The guy at the lab says any composite needs to go through a few touch-up phases.

ELEANOR So you're actually planning to use them.

MAXWELL Of course.

ELEANOR That's a criminal act.

MAXWELL I don't care.

[ELEANOR *gets his cane. Hands it to him*]

ELEANOR Here.

MAXWELL Thanks. [*He leaves.* ELEANOR *sighs. Starts to pick things up. Sighs. Takes some rubber cleaning gloves from her pocket. Puts them on. Picks up a bottle of cleaner from a corner somewhere. Looks at it. Sighs. Puts it down. Picks up the glass of water. And the bottle of pills. Goes to the couch. Looks at the pills*]

[*Blackout*]

Scene Six

Later

> ELEANOR *is asleep on the couch*
> *The office is still a mess*
> *Suddenly the conveyor is humming. And a large body wrapped in a pink drape is coming down on it from the street*
> MAXWELL, SARAH, *and* GAIL *come rushing in. Get to the conveyor as the body reaches the bottom. One of them hits the switch. It stops. They start to lift the body*

MAXWELL Careful. Don't drop him.

SARAH I've been trying to drop him all the way from the car.

GAIL Is that why you tried to trip me out on the street.

SARAH Yeah. Sorry.

MAXWELL Let's put him in that chair.
[*There is a chair next to the desk. They aim for it*]

SARAH Wow. This is one beefy white guy we got here. If the economy collapses and we're reduced to the worst possible scenario, the meat on this guy could feed us all for a year.

GAIL Sarah.

SARAH Just a passing thought. I mean, come on. Am I the only person who thinks about cannibalism from time to time. I doubt it!
[*They have the body in the chair*]

MAXWELL What's Eleanor doing.

GAIL Sleeping. It's three in the morning, Mr. Maxwell.

MAXWELL Really? I've lost track.... Look at her. I've never seen her asleep before. She looks so placid. I think she'd like us to wake her up though. I'm sure she'd want to be part of this.

SARAH I don't.

GAIL Me neither.
[SARAH *is picking up a pill bottle from the floor near* ELEANOR'*s outstretched hand*]

SARAH Besides, there's no waking her anyway. She took a couple of my pills. These things are lethal.

GAIL Does that mean she's going to die.

63

SARAH I meant lethal in the figurative sense ... whatever that means.

GAIL Does it mean she's just in a deep sleep.

SARAH Ah, yes. It does. Thank you.

MAXWELL Why do you suppose she took pills, Sarah.

SARAH I don't know. And until she changes her attitude to just about everything in the world, me included, I'm not sure I care.

GAIL What do we do with him.

MAXWELL I thought I told you what we're going to do with him.

GAIL I meant for now. Should we ... unwrap him.

SARAH I'm against that. Unless we cover up his eyes. His eyes are invitations to hell. He shot me a look while we were attacking him that turned my blood to ice. This is one beefy *evil* white guy we got here.... Leave him in his drape. It looks good. I like the colour. Pink is a very calming colour, did you know that. I wonder why a guy like this would have pink drapes. Why would he want to get calm.

MAXWELL Maybe it helps him think.

GAIL Think about really shitty stuff. Think about getting innocent kids to do his dirty work for him. Ruining their lives. God I hate him. I want to kick him. I really do.

SARAH Go ahead.

MAXWELL You don't have to kick him. You have other options now. You can bludgeon him with accountability.

GAIL When.

MAXWELL Soon.

GAIL How soon.

[HARRIS *comes on. In a trench coat. Under the trench coat, jogging pants and sweatshirt*]

HARRIS All right, Peter. What was that phone call all about. What's all this about.

MAXWELL [*to* GAIL] Starting now.

HARRIS You can't just call people at two in the morning with a bunch of veiled threats and think – [*points at body*] What's that.

MAXWELL [*to* GAIL] Uncover him.

[GAIL *starts to unwrap the body*]

SARAH Everything except his eyes.

Hardee T. Lineham (Harris), Peter Blais (Maxwell), Dawn Roach (Gail) and Nancy Beatty (Sarah)

MAXWELL No. He has to see. It's only fair. We're not barbarians.

SARAH Okay. But if he shoots me a look I can't be responsible for my actions.

HARRIS Is that who I think it is.

MAXWELL Yes.

HARRIS What did you do. Kidnap him?

MAXWELL Yes.

HARRIS Well you've done it now. There's no way out of this one, Peter. I'm getting the police.
[*SARAH rushes over. Blocks the door.* HARRIS *backs away from her.* GAIL *has* CONNER*'s head uncovered now. And is struggling to get the drape off his body.* CONNER *is unconscious. His mouth taped. His head drooping*]
Jesus. Look at him. Is he dead. Oh my God. [*points to* ELEANOR] Look at her. Is *she* dead. What is going on here. Are you people on some kind of rampage.

GAIL Yes.

MAXWELL Sean. [*he takes a step toward* HARRIS] Let me explain. There's a way out of this for everyone.

HARRIS Stay away from me. Why would you want to kill me, Peter. I've never done anything to you. All right so I've got your family. But you can have them back. Sandra, the kids, all of them. All right, so we don't agree politically anymore. But politics is compromise. We can work it out. If I'm elected I'll keep a – what's that thing?… Open mind. You and your friends will always have my ear. Listen. I'll even defend you. I'll go the stress route. Have it reduced to manslaughter. I know Conner probably drove you to it.… I don't know what Eleanor did to you but I'm sure it was hideous. Hideous.

MAXWELL Shut up! Calm down. Come on, calm down. No one's dead. Eleanor's just having a little nap. And we had to drug your friend Mr. Conner. It was the only way we could get him to come with us.

HARRIS Drugged him? Where'd you get the drugs. [SARAH *giggles*] From her?

SARAH Yes. I've got lots of them. Needles too. I'm an entirely self-contained pharmaceutical factory.

HARRIS You're a dope addict. I told Babe you were a dope addict. That's the only reason we didn't press charges against you for attacking him. We felt sorry for you.… I felt sorry for you too Peter. Reduced to practising law with junkies.…

MAXWELL Does anyone know what he's talking about.

SARAH I do. But I'm not telling.

HARRIS I'm getting out of here. Everyone stand back. I'm waking up Babe. And we're both leaving. Do you understand me. I'm being firm now.… If you don't cause any more trouble we might not call the police. We'll see how you do in the next few minutes.

MAXWELL Sit down, Sean!

[SARAH *and* GAIL *help* HARRIS *into a chair*]

The police are out of the question. We're not going that route. And when I'm finished explaining to you, I don't believe you'll want us to either. How did your announcement go. Were people enthusiastic. What do the early polls show. Do they look good? I bet they do, you old smoothy you. [*to others*] This guy's going to get elected. Does anyone in this room have a problem believing that.

GAIL I don't.

SARAH The self-destructive part of me would vote for him. The

socially conscious part of me would vote against him.
But the part of me I personally like the best, the part
that believes in primal justice, would throw him to the
floor, rip off his clothes and pour battery acid down his
rectum.

[MAXWELL *goes to* SARAH. *Touches her head. They nod at
each other momentarily.* MAXWELL *then turns back to*
HARRIS]

MAXWELL Well.... Well I wouldn't vote for him. I wouldn't elect
him to anything. He's a greedy prick. Aren't you, Sean.

HARRIS Depends on your point of view I suppose.

MAXWELL Come on admit it. You've admitted it to me before. Joked
and laughed about it in locker rooms many times.

HARRIS All right. I'm a greedy prick. So what.

MAXWELL Exactly. No I wouldn't vote for him. But thousands will.
Well he just ... looks ... so damn good. I'd say he's a
shoo-in. Unless of course, there's a ripple. [*points to*
CONNER] He could be your ripple, Sean. Don't say I didn't
warn you.

HARRIS What are you talking about.

MAXWELL He's a crook. [*to* GAIL] Isn't he.

GAIL Yes.

MAXWELL We've got proof. [*to* SARAH] Haven't we.

SARAH Yes.

MAXWELL He's a proven crook. And he's your crook. Just like
you're his candidate. There was a picture in the paper
of you together at your announcement. Hands clasped.
Arms raised. It was a lovely picture. It made me feel
great. When I saw it I knew I had you.

HARRIS How.

MAXWELL That picture bonds the two of you in the public's eye.

HARRIS What do you want from me, Peter.

MAXWELL The first thing is this. We want you out of politics. We
don't want you running this country Sean. You're a
greedy prick. And maybe that's all right for you and your
friends, but hey, they're greedy pricks too. And we've
already got enough of them to deal with. So you're not
going to seek public office. Do you agree to that.

HARRIS No, I don't.

MAXWELL You must want it very badly. That makes me feel great.

I'll tell you why in a minute. Second thing is, we want you to get Gail's husband out of prison.

HARRIS Why. Is he important to you for some reason.

GAIL He's innocent.

HARRIS [*laughs*] Sure he is.

[GAIL *advances on him*]

HARRIS No. Sure. He is!

MAXWELL Listen to her Sean. Personally, I've decided to restrict the word innocent to descriptions of angels and newborn babies. Let's just say he's not guilty of the crime for which he was convicted.

GAIL Conner's guys, his guys, sent Dave into one of the other newspaper's warehouses. To smash up some machinery. They sent him into another one's office to steal some advertising information or something. They told him if he didn't do it, they'd come after *me* and hurt *me*.

MAXWELL In our newly revised way of looking at things, the law included, that makes Dave not guilty. Get him out. I don't care how. Get him an appeal. Use your connections. Or have Conner send his own guys up for some time. Like I said I don't care. Just get it done. We'll be monitoring your progress on this, Sean.

HARRIS First I want to know what you have connecting Mr. Conner to these alleged criminals.

MAXWELL Pictures.

HARRIS Okay. I want to see them.

MAXWELL No you don't. You know I've got them. You know me well enough to know I wouldn't enter into the fray unprepared. I mean I'm a new man, Sean. But some old habits are worth keeping.

HARRIS Well, nevertheless it could be difficult. These things take a certain amount –

MAXWELL We're off that subject, Sean. We're moving on. [*to* GAIL] How's Mr. Conner.

GAIL He's coming to.

[GAIL *rips the tape from* CONNER's *mouth.* SARAH *takes a rope from her knapsack. Begins to tie* CONNER *to his chair*]

MAXWELL What we want you to do now is the big test. If you do it

Love And Anger

well we could resolve this dilemma without anyone
getting seriously hurt. Without your reputation getting
seriously hurt. And therefore any chance you have of
getting elected. Do you understand.

HARRIS Yes.

MAXWELL Good boy. But you'll have to do your best. No sloughing
off. None of that famous disdain for the fanciful they've
all grown to love at your club.

HARRIS Yes, yes. What is it.

MAXWELL A trial.

HARRIS A what.

MAXWELL A trial.

HARRIS Whose trial.

[MAXWELL *points at* CONNER]

MAXWELL His.

HARRIS For what. For those break-ins?

MAXWELL No no. That's small potatoes. We can live with our
earlier resolution to that injustice. This is bigger. More
... more....

SARAH Cosmic. In an urban sense.

MAXWELL Yes. And also more satisfying. He is going to stand trial
for his newspaper, for his public stands on all the major
issues of the day, on his contributions to making this
city a place which is only satisfying to baseball fans and
real estate agents! For his endless manipulative use of
the lowest common denominator and his lack of
respect for the essential mysteries of life!

SARAH The official charge is: Being ... Consciously ... Evil.

MAXWELL [*to* HARRIS] And you are defending him. It's a simple
win – lose situation. If we win he closes his newspaper.
If you win, we don't go public with proof that your
friend is a low-life crook.

GAIL But he still has to get Dave out no matter what.

MAXWELL That's a given.

SARAH Let's get started.

[GAIL *and* SARAH *start to tidy up a bit. Move the desk more
centre. And rearrange the chairs.* CONNER *stirs. Moans. In
a daze*]

CONNER Hey. Where am I.

GAIL In court.

69

SARAH On trial for your life.

HARRIS His life? What does she mean by that.

MAXWELL She was probably speaking figuratively. She often does.... Were you speaking figuratively Sarah.

SARAH No I was trying to scare the shit out of him. I don't like him.

MAXWELL You see, Sean? Just an honest expression of simple human feelings.

GAIL [to MAXWELL] How are you feeling, Mr. Maxwell.

MAXWELL I'll get through it. Maybe I should just sit down for a moment though. Get prepared.
[He sits on the couch]

HARRIS Surely you don't seriously expect me to go along with this, Peter.

MAXWELL I'm sorry, but you don't have a choice. I warned you to break your ties to this guy. And now your reputation is at stake. And because you're a man without a soul, your reputation is the only thing you have. Relax. All you have to do is win. Winning is second nature to you.

HARRIS Of all the demented, screwed up, harebrained, pathetic half-baked ideas – a trial. A goddamn trial!? Who are you. God? No. You're nothing. You're a sick old man with delusions of grandeur. You're pitiful. You're living the life of a fool. You're surrounded by fools. Pathetic. Why are you doing this to me. Why? Because I'm a greedy prick? You were a greedy prick too. For twenty years you were one of the greediest and one of the biggest!

MAXWELL I repented.
[HARRIS sits on the couch next to MAXWELL. They have to roll the sleeping ELEANOR on her side to make room]

HARRIS You can't. You can't repent just like that. That's not how it works. Even I know that.

MAXWELL Yes you can. You just say to yourself 'I repent.' You send a message out to the world that you're sorry for what you've been. Any kind of message.

HARRIS Okay. I repent too.

MAXWELL Too late!

HARRIS Says who.

MAXWELL [standing] Me! Me! The demigod. The former greedy

70

prick. The man with a hole in his brain. The angry man.
The reborn man. The avenger! I warned you didn't I....
The avenger is here. And it's me!!

HARRIS Come on. Get a hold of yourself. It's not too late to
stop –

MAXWELL Shut up! [*smiles*] I'm preparing. I'd advise you to do the
same, Sean. I'd advise you to get deadly serious about
this right now! Confer with your client if you wish.
[CONNER *stirs again*]

CONNER Hey. Is this a dream.

SARAH Yeah. And it's beautiful.
[SARAH *is staring off into the distance*]

MAXWELL Everyone take a minute. Gather your thoughts. This is a
monumental task we're about to undertake.

GAIL Yeah. I feel like praying or something.

MAXWELL Good idea. Everyone look inside your head. Locate your
individual God. Have a few words.
[CONNER *stands. Notices that he is still tied to the chair*]

CONNER Jesus Christ!

SARAH Typical choice.
[*Blackout*]

Scene Seven

A moment or two later
   The basic courtroom set-up
   SARAH *is the judge. She is sitting behind the desk.*
*Wearing the pink drape around her shoulders. In front,
and to one side of her,* GAIL *is taking notes, as the court
stenographer.* ELEANOR *is still asleep on the couch*
   Down to the right of the desk a chair for MAXWELL.
Down and to the left two chairs – one for HARRIS, *one for*
CONNER, *who is still tied to the chair. And is gagged again*
   The scene begins in darkness. Except for a light on
SARAH. *Yelling*

SARAH Order. Order. Order in the court. I'll have order. Give it
to me. I want it. It's mine! Orderrrrr!

71

[*Lights up on an argument. Both* HARRIS *and* MAXWELL *are leaning on the desk.* SARAH *is on her feet*]

HARRIS There are no rules here! Where are the rules!

MAXWELL To hell with the rules! We don't need –

HARRIS This is anarchy! I can't work this way.

SARAH Order! [*to* HARRIS] You. Sit down or I'll have you put in handcuffs. What are you doing here anyway.

HARRIS I'm the lawyer for the defendant!

SARAH That's the spirit! [*smiles*] Just checking. [*to* MAXWELL] He's committed. We can proceed. You're out of order too by the way. Sit down.

HARRIS What's she going on about. When did the trial begin. Who made her judge. See what I mean? No rules!

MAXWELL Wing it. Speak from the heart, man.

HARRIS Well what's the framework. Common law?

MAXWELL Let's not be parochial. We've got choices you know. Even within the common law. British, Canadian, American.

SARAH The only trials I've seen have been on TV.

MAXWELL It'll have to be American then.

SARAH We'll make it up. We'll do fine. Just be nice boys. Try to get along. [*to* GAIL] Are you getting all this.

GAIL You're going too fast.

SARAH Don't write it down verbatim. Just aim for the essence. You're a born writer, honey. Just do your thing.

MAXWELL And remember you're writing for posterity. Don't worry about the structure. But use lots of imagery. [*to* HARRIS] That okay with you?

HARRIS I want my client ungagged.

SARAH We tried that. But he started to talk. What he said made the court nauseous. He'll be allowed to testify on his own behalf.

HARRIS That's big of you.

SARAH That's big of you, what.

HARRIS I don't know. What!?

SARAH That's big of you, *Your Honour*. You watch it now. I'll hold you in contempt. And you don't want to know what being held in contempt means in my court. Got that?

HARRIS Yes … your honour.

SARAH   Good boy. [*to* MAXWELL] Present your case.

MAXWELL   Thank you, Your Honour. On behalf of the people I wish to –

HARRIS   I…. He…. I mean…. Objection, Your *Honour*. He has no right to claim he represents the people. Who are the people. The people here? An amorphous mass outside…. I mean come on –

MAXWELL   I use the term 'the people' quite correctly, Your Honour. Societal crimes have been committed and the victims of these crimes are in fact –

SARAH   Yeah yeah. Objection overruled. [*to* HARRIS] Calm down. It's just a word. People. I can relate to what he means. Don't worry. This court isn't too crazy about 'the people' anyway. He doesn't get any advantage saying shit like that around me. [*to* MAXWELL] Continue. No wait. Something's wrong. I think I should be higher. In a position to look down on you all. I think the looking down thing is essential here. [*she grabs a waste can. Puts it on the desk. Sits on it*] This feels better. [*to* GAIL] How's it look.

GAIL   I just wrote that you look like a primitive warrior. A kind of furious but wise queen. Like someone in the Bible.

SARAH   She's a genius. [*to* MAXWELL] Well, what are you waiting for. Speak.

MAXWELL   We will attempt to prove that the accused, knowingly and with total disregard for the consequences, pursued a career injurious to the public well-being. That he –

HARRIS   Objection. That's impossible to prove.

SARAH   Well why not let him be the judge of that. It's his job after all.

HARRIS   Very well. It's impossible to defend against.

SARAH   Try. Maybe you'll surprise yourself.

HARRIS   So what you're getting at here, Peter – what upsets you – if you'll allow me to put it in terms that a mere mortal like myself – someone not in touch with God's true purpose on earth – can understand, is that you don't like the choice of headlines in the guy's newspaper. You don't like – what? – his view of the world, or something.

MAXWELL   Oh for God's sake. I don't *like* butterscotch ice cream. I don't *like* people who only talk seriously about foreign

films. This guy, this buddy of yours is an enemy of the
human race. So what I'm *getting* at, what *upsets* me
about his newspaper is that it promotes the theory of
the survival of the fittest. The law of the jungle. And the
problem with that is actually very simple to understand.
This is not a jungle! It's a civilization! Get it? Get the
difference? Well your buddy doesn't, or for some very
cynical reason he chooses not to. And that is why I
despise him from the bottom of my soul.

HARRIS Yes, but what has he *done*?! What has he actually done
that he has to defend himself. To anyone. To any court.
Even to this sorry excuse for a court.

SARAH Be careful.

MAXWELL You heard the charge.

HARRIS Being evil? What's that mean. That's purely subjective.

MAXWELL No, it's a matter of consensus.

HARRIS But how are you going to prove it!

MAXWELL Well just watch me, you silly bastard!

HARRIS I'd like a moment to confer with my client.

SARAH Go ahead. But be quick about it.

HARRIS Don't push me! I can only be pushed so far!

SARAH You think so? Well I'll push your asshole through your
brain until you're inside out in another fucking universe!
The universe of the brainless assholes! Don't ever
fucking tell me how far I can push someone! It's bad for
my fucking health! Bad for everyone's fucking health! It's
bad therapy! Bad karma! Bad fucking manners!!

HARRIS Oh please. Help me out here Peter. I can't deal with her
at all. I can't. I just ... fucking can't!

MAXWELL Just talk to your client if you're going to talk to him! I
haven't got all day, man!
[HARRIS *goes over to* CONNER. *Whispers to him.* CONNER
begins to nod]

GAIL How are you feeling, Mr. Maxwell.

MAXWELL To be honest.... Not great.

GAIL You look a bit pale.

MAXWELL Headache. A pretty bad one. And I think it's growing. I
wish he'd hurry up over there. I don't know how much
time I've got. Come on, Sean!

HARRIS I wish to make a suggestion ... Your *Honour*. I think we should skip the opening ... statements. I've talked to my client and he agrees to testify at this point in time. He also promises not to make any undue fuss. This way Mr. Maxwell here can proceed with direct interrogation and I will have a recognizable structure to operate within. Agreed?

SARAH Agreed.

MAXWELL Agreed.

[HARRIS *starts to untie* CONNER. ELEANOR *stands up. Stretches*]

ELEANOR Oh well that was a sleep to remember. Those pills are something – [*looks around*] What are you doing up there, Sarah! Please get down. [*to others*] Has there been an incident. I'm so sorry.

SARAH Hey. I didn't do anything wrong. Just go back to sleep. Everything is fine.

MAXWELL Come over here, Eleanor. Take my chair.
[*She does*]

ELEANOR What's going on.

SARAH Just do what he says. Listen. Watch. You might learn something.

MAXWELL [*helping her into the chair*] I might need you to assist me. I'm not feeling that –

ELEANOR Why. What's wrong with you.
[CONNER *is free. He attacks* MAXWELL]

CONNER Okay. What's stopping me from pounding the shit out of all of you right now.

MAXWELL [*to* HARRIS] I thought you explained to him.
[HARRIS *pulls* CONNER *off* MAXWELL]

HARRIS I did. [*to* CONNER] Take the stand, Babe. We've both got too much at stake here.

CONNER Oh I'll take the stand all right. I'll take the stand and wrap it around this asshole's skull. Then I'll take the pieces and ram them down the throat of that crazy bitch up there.

HARRIS This won't help, Babe. Like I told you they have –

CONNER Yeah I know. They've got some proof about some little thing. But shit. They broke into my house. They attacked me. They put needles in my arm. They threw me in the trunk of a car. This is some kind of fucking nightmare.

75

Peter Blais (Maxwell), Clare Coulter (Eleanor), Dawn Roach (Gail), Nancy Beatty (Sarah), Benedict Campbell (Conner), and Hardee T. Lineham (Harris)

Dawn Roach (Gail), Peter Blais (Maxwell), Nancy Beatty (Sarah), Benedict Campbell (Conner), and Hardee T. Lineham (Harris)

What did I ever do to these people. And I have to take this shit? I have to sit down and take this abuse from these people. Why. I'm asking you why.

HARRIS I told you why!

CONNER I know! But it doesn't seem like enough of a reason. It's like I want a better reason. It's almost like I want to ask God for a reason. I feel that fucked up about this thing. Jesus! I'm a citizen of some standing in this community.

MAXWELL You're a thieving, conniving, merciless, exploiting piece of sewage!

CONNER I am not!

MAXWELL Prove it!

HARRIS & CONNER How!

SARAH & MAXWELL Take the stand!

CONNER Yeah. Okay. Okay yeah. I'll take it. Where is it. I'll take it. Then you'll see. I'm not afraid. Jesus. Where is the fucking *stand*!

SARAH That chair down there. Next to me.
[CONNER *goes to chair. Sits. Weeps*]

CONNER [*to* HARRIS] Did you hear the names that guy called me. They were horrible. Just rotten. [*looks up*] God. It's me. Sorry to bother you. But what's goin' on here.

ELEANOR [*to* MAXWELL] Is this what I think it is, Peter.

MAXWELL A trial. Yes.

ELEANOR Oh dear.
[ELEANOR *stands.* MAXWELL *sits*]

HARRIS [*to* SARAH] I suppose you want to swear him in, in your own inimitable fashion.

SARAH Yeah. [*to* CONNER] You're going to be asked some questions. Are you going to lie.

CONNER No!

SARAH Oh sure. We really believe that.

HARRIS That's prejudicial. I want another judge.

CONNER So do I.

SARAH I was just expressing my true feelings. I think it best if the court is honest about these things. It doesn't mean I can't be turned around or anything. You guys have forgotten almost all the important things about life haven't you.

HARRIS Make Eleanor the judge. She's a fair person.

SARAH [*mocking*] 'Make Eleanor the judge.' 'Make Eleanor the judge.' 'She's fair. She's coherent. She's neat. She's normal.' No way. It ain't gonna happen. I'm here. And I'm staying. You hear that Eleanor? So stop promoting yourself for my job. [*she starts to cry*] Just stop it!

ELEANOR I don't want the job, Sarah. Believe me.

SARAH Oh you're lobbying for it all right. Standing there the way you do. Standing there all rational. And deferential. Looking perfect for the position. Just waiting for the chance to serve.

[*The next three speeches come simultaneously*]

ELEANOR Don't Sarah. You're getting yourself all worked up. It just won't do, so stop it!

GAIL Leave her alone. She's a good judge. She's doing just fine.

MAXWELL Please, my head. Please! Sarah's the judge!

[*Pause*]

CONNER [*looking up*] Are you hearing all this God. This is the thanks I get for being a good citizen? Making my contribution? Providing over three hundred jobs? This is my reward? Putting my fate in the hands of these lunatics? Oh man I'm confused by this. I'm right on the edge here. [*he drops to his knees, closes his eyes, begins to pray*] Oh Lord. Give me your wisdom here. Pass it along, Lord. Help me defeat my enemies. Help me find my way back into the light. Help me stay prosperous and productive. Dear Jesus. Help me crush these assholes. Help me to –

[*About halfway into* CONNER's *prayer,* ELEANOR *advances and stands above him silently. Now she quickly takes off her rubber cleaning gloves and begins to slap* CONNER *with them.* CONNER *hides behind* HARRIS. *And* ELEANOR *is slapping them both.*]

Hey! Hey what the fuck. Jesus.... Hey....

ELEANOR How dare you talk to God like that! How dare you ask God to save your miserable hide. You leave God out of this. The nerve of you asking him to keep you prosperous when there's so much real pain in the world! [*she starts back to her chair*]

78

CONNER [*jumping up*] Okay. That's enough. She hit me. She's gonna die! [*he starts after her*]

[SARAH *throws off the drape and jumps on his back.* GAIL *jumps and puts a head lock on him.* HARRIS *and* MAXWELL *join in to separate them. They form a mass of bodies and collapse on the couch in a tangle*]

HARRIS No! No no. Not again. Come on now.

MAXWELL Sarah. Gail. This isn't the way.

HARRIS Get them off him.

MAXWELL I'm trying. Help me. Please!

[*They are all groaning. Talking. Finally* CONNER *gets free. Stands. The rest of them are on the couch. Except* ELEANOR *who remains in her chair. Looking worried. And angry*]

CONNER This is what I mean. This is the perfect defense. Where do you people get the right to judge anyone. You're a bunch of screw-ups. You've got me on your own terrain. You've taken away all my rights. Taken me away from a world where I have status. And you still can't pull it off. You're pathetic!

ELEANOR No they're not! They're just struggling. Struggling to replace a ... a ... system that has let them down for some reason. Be nice to them! They're only looking for a little justice.

[CONNER *goes to* ELEANOR]

CONNER I've done nothing wrong! I didn't know those punks were going to pull that rough stuff. I was engaged in a little industrial espionage. It gets done to me all the time.

ELEANOR Well at least now you're admitting it. Did you hear that, Peter. He's admitting it.

CONNER What's the point of denying it. He's got pictures of me with those two bozos hasn't he.

ELEANOR Yes he has. And don't you forget it!

CONNER What's the fuss. It's just a little crime. It happens all the time. Everyone does it. It's part of the game. Part of the real world.

[SARAH *stands*]

SARAH Real to who? It's not real to me. It's an obscene fantasy to me. People managing and arranging. People being managed and getting arranged. Just thinking about it makes me want to vomit.

[HARRIS *stands*]

HARRIS We don't care how you feel about it. You're not capable of taking part in it. You're obviously a very ill person. I feel sorry for you. It's because I feel sorry for you that I'm willing to subsidize your medical expenses.

CONNER [*to* SARAH] Subsidize! Yeah. I hire celebrities to entertain people like you in the hospital. My ex-wife is a fundraiser for that hospital. She does it because she cares and because I pay her alimony, she's got the time to care. I love this country. I love this city. My contributions to this city are legendary. I support the opera.

HARRIS So do I.

[SARAH *is between them. Looking at each in turn. Wide-eyed. Incredulous*]

CONNER I support the United Appeal.

HARRIS So do I.

CONNER I support the Boy Scouts, the Girl Guides and *three* day care centres. I sponsor a little league team, two bantam hockey leagues.

HARRIS I sponsor one of those too.

CONNER I promote the building of sports facilities in this city. Sports are very important. They help keep people healthy.

HARRIS People who want to be healthy. People who aren't afraid to meet life head on.

CONNER People who want to be successful.

HARRIS You bet.

[*And now* CONNER *and* HARRIS *talking only to each other. Joyfully. Passionately*]

CONNER Successful on the right terms.

HARRIS The terms of a true consensus. They're the foundation of our society, those people and their consensus. It's a prosperous society. Deny that.

CONNER No way. I can't.

HARRIS I mean compare it to any other society. Sure there are people who get left out. That's a pity. There are people living on the street. But overall –

CONNER Fuck the people living on the fucking street. I've heard enough about the fucking people on the street. I mean you'd think there were thousands of them, the kind of press they get. I mean Jesus man this has got to be a place for winners. We've got to keep the momentum going. Let the slower people pick up the jet stream. That's our only choice. We've got to get richer. The only alternative is to get poorer.

HARRIS I love this man! [*points at* CONNER] This is a brave man.

CONNER Thank you.

[*They hug. They pat each other on the back. They're on the verge of tears*]

HARRIS No. Thank *you*. Thank you for your courage and your contributions. And your spunky little newspaper that gives people what they need. And thank you for hiring me. And getting your friends to hire me. And helping me stay rich. [*he stands on the desk*] And thereby allowing me to run for public office and thereby helping me help everyone else become rich. [*to others*] Rich is good.

[CONNER *buries his head in* HARRIS' *crotch*]

It's good. It's very very good!

[*A noise up on the street. Garbage cans rattling.* MAXWELL *stands. Starts toward the window*]

MAXWELL Hey you! I've told you not to eat that garbage! [*to others*] They won't stop. I've asked. I've pleaded.... They just won't stop!

SARAH Time for the verdict. Guilty. Both of them. I sentence them to death by drowning. In the toilet. Let's get them down to the washroom.

CONNER Back off!

SARAH You back off!

CONNER I mean it!

SARAH He means it! I'll fucking show you what meaning it means.

[*She advances quickly on* CONNER]

MAXWELL Stop it, just stop it! Get them out of my sight. They won. I lost my fire. I'm sorry, okay! I think I'm dying.

[ELEANOR *and* GAIL *go to* MAXWELL. *Help him into a chair*]

SARAH All right. [*to* HARRIS] If he says so – you won.

CONNER We know. We could feel it. We recognized the feeling, didn't we Sean.

HARRIS Definitely.

81

SARAH Don't push your luck. I'm letting you go out of respect for a dying man. A man I love.

HARRIS No police, Peter? No press? Nothing about the break-ins?

ELEANOR Hey. He's a man of his word. You should at least know that!

GAIL Just make sure you get my husband out of prison.

SARAH We'll be monitoring you.

ELEANOR Remember, we've still got those pictures. And they're great pictures.

HARRIS Come on, Babe.

[HARRIS *picks up the pink drape. Puts it around* CONNER'S *shoulders*]

CONNER Sure.... So this was just an argument right.... I mean if you leave out the rough stuff. Kind of ... a debate. And we beat the crap out them. Looking back it was kind of exciting.

[*They start off*]

GAIL There's something I'd like to add to the argument.

[*They turn. Look at her. Laugh. Start off again.* GAIL *takes a small gun from her pocket. Fires it in the air. They stop*]

CONNER [*turns*] Jesus.

HARRIS What's this. Peter, what's she doing.

MAXWELL Gail.

ELEANOR Please. Not a gun. Anything but a gun. [*to* MAXWELL] Ask her why she has a gun.

GAIL The first time I met this guy, he attacked me remember. I wasn't going to be in a room with him again without any protection. It's not that I didn't believe in you Mr. Maxwell. I've just learned to be prepared.

HARRIS So what do you want.

GAIL Like I said. I just wanted to add something to the argument.

CONNER Yeah, what?

[GAIL *holds up the gun*]

GAIL This. It's real.

HARRIS We know.

GAIL You see I've been listening.... Mr. Maxwell didn't lose his fire. He's just a gentle man at heart. Or maybe he's just forgetful. Anyway he left something out of the argument.

And this is it. The gun. See it? If you cross me or my husband again, I'll use it. If you make me mad again I'll find you and put it against your head and pull the trigger. Maybe because I think you're wrong about all the things you talked about. Maybe for ... some other reasons. We'll never know for sure why I use it. I'll never know because I'll be too busy getting on with my life to ask myself questions like that. And you'll never know because you'll be dead....

[HARRIS *and* CONNER *look at each other*]

HARRIS Well you've really ticked *her* off.

CONNER And I don't even know who she is.... Anyway she was talking to both of us.

HARRIS No way.

CONNER Ask her.

HARRIS I don't want to.

GAIL Hey.... You can leave now.

[*They turn. Leave*]

ELEANOR Gail. Where did you get that gun.

SARAH I gave it to her.... I've had it for quite awhile. Just in case.

ELEANOR Just in case what.

SARAH Just in case I had to use it.... You know? Use it? [*she uses her fingers as a gun, puts it to her head, pulls the trigger*]

ELEANOR Oh my God.

GAIL What's it matter how I got it. I've just got it. And those guys know I've got it.

[MAXWELL *stands*]

MAXWELL Gail. It's an honour to have known you. [*to others*] She is your leader. Follow her to the ... promised....

[*He collapses into* ELEANOR's *arms. She sinks to her knees*]

Eleanor, is my will on file. I want to bequeath some money to Sarah and Gail.

ELEANOR You don't have any money, Peter. You gave it all away, remember.

MAXWELL Ah yes. [*to* SARAH *and* GAIL] Well I was thinking of you. Trust me. It really is the thought ... that counts....

Eleanor, you look like my mother.

[SARAH *is backing away*]

ELEANOR You never told me that.

83

MAXWELL You never looked like her before.... Until just ... this moment.

SARAH I don't know why he's talking like this. Or why he looks the way he does. Am I supposed to be worried here. I don't feel very well.

MAXWELL Sarah. Come here.

SARAH No. I can't.

MAXWELL Please.

[SARAH *is rubbing the floor with one foot*]

SARAH No. I'm ... I'm ... doing something. I'm very busy here at the moment. Maybe later. We'll talk. Have lunch or something.... I don't know.

MAXWELL She's scared.

ELEANOR Who isn't.

MAXWELL Oh Lord. I've let you all down haven't I.

ELEANOR Yes.

GAIL No.

ELEANOR I'm sorry. I meant to say no. Honestly. You did fine Peter. You had those men very very scared there for awhile.

MAXWELL Didn't want to ... scare them. Wanted to dazzle them. Turn them inside out. I was naive, right?

ELEANOR Yes.

GAIL No.

ELEANOR Yes. Damn it! Yes. Naive! Unbelievably dangerously naive! ... I'm sorry....

MAXWELL It's all right. In some cases naive is preferable.... But not this time. I left it too late. My rebirth. Tried to ... cram it all in.... I should have started earlier. When I was younger ... spread the anger out a ... bit.
[*He dies.* ELEANOR *lays him down gently*]

SARAH What are you doing. Don't put him down on the floor like that.

ELEANOR He's dead.

SARAH Who says.

ELEANOR He stopped breathing.

SARAH Well maybe he'll start again.

ELEANOR Sarah.

SARAH Don't start. I don't want to hear any of your coherent talk, Eleanor. Just pick up his head. Hold it for awhile. Cradle it. Give the guy a chance to reconsider. Maybe

he's just weighing his options. Show him you love him
Eleanor. Maybe he'll come back to us. Why do you give
up so easily, Eleanor. Why won't you just pick up the
poor guy's head.

ELEANOR [*to* GAIL] Can you help me explain to her.

GAIL Pick up his head, Eleanor. What have you got to lose. It
might make you feel good....
[ELEANOR *sighs. Lifts* MAXWELL's *head. Puts it in her lap*]

SARAH Massage his head a bit. Really gently. Gently. Gently.

ELEANOR How long do you want me to do this, Sarah.

SARAH I don't know. For as long as it takes I guess. I've never
brought anyone back from the dead before. It could take
hours. Weeks.... I think he's worth it though. Worth the
effort.... [*to* GAIL] Don't you.

GAIL Yes.

SARAH I mean the guy had something. He was on to something.
[*to* GAIL] Don't you think?

GAIL Yes. I do.

ELEANOR I can't keep doing this, Sarah. It's wrong. It's making me
feel so –

SARAH I need him Eleanor. I need him back. He created an
environment that was good for me. He made a
connection in my head. His anger connected to my
anger. It blotted out the voices.
[GAIL *puts her hand on* SARAH's *shoulder*]

GAIL I can do that. I can do that for you.

SARAH Yeah?

GAIL Yeah.... I think so.

SARAH So ... well ... what can I do for you.

GAIL You're great. It's just great to be around you. We'll just
be friends. It'll be exciting for me. You're the most
amazing person I've ever met.

SARAH Yeah? You hear that Eleanor?

ELEANOR Yes.

SARAH We're going to be friends. [*to* GAIL] You're not saying all
this just because we're the same colour, are you.

GAIL No.

SARAH You hear that, Eleanor? She and I are really going to be
friends. And it's going to be exciting. What do you think
of that.

ELEANOR I don't know.

SARAH Well at least she's not against it.

[ELEANOR *and* GAIL *look at* SARAH. *Then all three look down at* MAXWELL*'s body. Concentrate*]

[*Lights fade to black*]

[*End*]

Other published plays by George F. Walker

Ambush at Tether's End. In *The Factory Lab Anthology* (ed. Connie Brissenden). Vancouver: Talonbooks, 1974.

The East End Plays. Toronto: Playwrights Canada, 1988. Includes *Beautiful City, Better Living,* and *Criminals in Love.*

Nothing Sacred. Toronto: Coach House Press, 1988.

The Power Plays. Toronto: Coach House Press, 1984. Includes *The Art of War, Filthy Rich,* and *Gossip.*

Rumours of Our Death. In *Canadian Theatre Review* 25 (Winter, 1980), pp. 43-72.

Science and Madness. Toronto: Playwrights Canada, 1972.

Theatre of the Film Noir. Toronto: Playwrights Canada, 1981.

Three Plays. Toronto: Coach House Press, 1978. Includes *Bagdad Saloon, Beyond Mozambique,* and *Ramona and the White Slaves.*

Zastrozzi. Toronto: Playwrights Canada, 1979.

Zastrozzi: The Master of Discipline. In *Modern Canadian Plays* (ed. Jerry Wasserman). Vancouver: Talonbooks, 1985.

Editor for the press: Robert Wallace
Photographs: Nir Bareket
Cover design: Gordon Robertson
Text design: Nelson Adams

For a list of our drama titles, or to
receive a catalogue, write to:

Coach House Press
401 (rear) Huron Street
Toronto, Canada M5S 2G5